THE AP......

004852

THE APARTMENT

Billy Wilder
and
I. A. L. Diamond

faber and faber

First published in 1998
by Faber and Faber Limited
3 Queen Square London WC1N 3AU

Photoset by Parker Typesetting Service, Leicester
Printed in England by Clays Ltd, St Ives plc

Billy Wilder and I. A. L. Diamond are hereby identified as
authors of this work in accordance with Section 77 of the Copyright,
Designs and Patents Act 1988

A CIP record for this book
is available from the British Library

ISBN 0-571-19409-5

2 4 6 8 10 9 7 5 3 1

CONTENTS

INTRODUCTION

The seeds of the idea for *The Apartment* were sewn thirteen years before its shooting script was completed. When Billy Wilder saw David Lean's 1945 film *Brief Encounter*, about a middle-class love affair between a housewife and a doctor, he began to wonder about one of the minor characters. As he told Michel Ciment, 'The lovers meet in the apartment of a friend of the hero. I think that the interesting character is the friend who returns to his home and finds the bed still warm, he who has no mistress.'

In late 1958, when *Some Like it Hot* was completed but not released, Wilder and his regular co-writer I.A.L. Diamond returned to this nugget of an idea and started fleshing out the *Brief Encounter* character. In his biography of Wilder, *Wilder Times*, Kevin Lally says that 'the memory of a 1951 Hollywood scandal helped crystallise the idea'. An unmarried employee of film producer Walter Wanger had, apparently, provided his boss with a love nest. 'What if the lending of the apartment wasn't an act of friendship,' says Lally, 'but a career move? Now the concept had a little edge – something to do with what it takes to get ahead in corporate America.' Tony Curtis, who'd just worked for Wilder on *Some Like it Hot*, says in his autobiography that *The Apartment* idea came from another source. A friend of his lent his apartment to married friends for secret affairs. 'Columnist Sidney Skolsky,' says Lally of the Curtis account, 'heard about the arrangement, wrote it up as a movie treatment and sold it to Wilder.'

Whichever of these is true, Wilder and Diamond now had a character and a theme and set to work. Their routine was as it had been when writing *Love in the Afternoon* and *Some Like it Hot*. As Wilder described it in 1988, after Diamond's death: 'Iz and I are more like bank tellers. We open the shop at nine-thirty, there is a quick exchange of "morning, morning", I'd sit at my desk, he'd slouch in the black chair, his feet on the ottoman, chewing gum. Sometimes the muses would come and kiss our brow and we'd whip up ten or twelve pages per day, Iz on the typewriter, me on the yellow pad. There was no arm-twisting, pulling rank, shouting or screaming . . . when one came up with an idea that wasn't too bad. The highest accolade you could get out of Iz was "Why not?" '

They were complimentary personalities, with similar roots. Wilder did everything in a rush. Diamond was introverted. Viennese Wilder went to West Coast America in 1933, at the age of twenty-seven. Romanian Diamond (born Itek Dommnici) went to East Coast America before Wilder, in 1929, at the age of just nine. While it's easy to see Wilder's mix of German and English in Mrs Dreyfuss's great Baxter put-down speech ('Mit the drinking, mit the cha-cha, mit the no napkins', p. 113), it is said that Diamond contributed the New York street talk to *The Apartment* (such as landlady Mrs Lieberman's: 'Mr Baxter, open up already!' p. 100).

Wilder first noticed Diamond because of the sketches he wrote for a Writer's Guild dinner. He had written light comedies for Jack Carson at Warners and been a script doctor on films such as *Three Coins in a Fountain* and *There's No Business Like Show Business*. In 1955, Wilder was finishing *The Spirit of St Louis* and needed someone to start on *Love in the Afternoon*. *The Spirit of St Louis* overran, so Wilder and Diamond didn't sit down together to complete the next picture until spring 1956. Their collaboration lasted twenty-five years, for twelve films.

The Apartment was to be Wilder's first film from an original screenplay since *Ace in the Hole* in 1951. With no source material the writers started literally with a blank sheet, on which Wilder wrote *'cum deo'* (with God). They knew that their film would be shot in Panavision so a scene could run for several pages of dialogue; Wilder didn't like a lot of cutting and the wide image allowed him to photograph several people within the frame, talking to each other.

Wilder cast as they wrote. Baxter was always to be played by Jack Lemmon. The director called him 'the most consummate and appealing actor since the early Chaplin'. He felt that with Lemmon audiences would never lose sympathy with the careerist, number-crunching insurance man. Marilyn Monroe said that she wanted to play Fran. She was about the same age as Lemmon (mid-thirties), whereas Shirley MacLaine was only twenty-five, but MacLaine had just been stunning in *Some Came Running*, for which she'd won an Oscar nomination, and Wilder had just finished doing forty takes with Monroe in *Some Like it Hot*. MacLaine says that by the time she started on *The Apartment*, she'd only seen twenty-nine pages, but that she 'admired the social statement Billy was making and the extraordinary sophistication he brought to making that statement'.

Sheldrake was to have been played by Paul Douglas, but he died suddenly of a heart attack before shooting began. When Wilder then went to Fred MacMurray, the latter was uncertain about playing a conniving adulterer, as he had been about playing the equally amoral character of Walter Neff in Wilder's *Double Indemnity*, sixteen years earlier. By the time of *The Apartment*, MacMurray was under contract to Disney and slated to do *The Absent-Minded Professor*. He was a light comedian who thought he'd never be forgiven for playing the rat Sheldrake. 'Everything is possible,' said Wilder, 'if you've just got a certain amount of charm.'

Filming began in November 1959 at Central Park, West 69th Street and at the Majestic Theater on 44th Street. It ran for four months. The budget was about $3 million. The sets, which were built on the Goldwyn lot, cost $400,000. The biggest of these was that of the 19th floor of Consolidated Life. Billy Wilder had seen King Vidor's 1928 film *The Crowd* while still in Europe, and remembered Cedric Gibbons' vast perspective office where James Murray's character worked. He asked the great Jewish Hungarian art director Alexander Trauner, who'd done the sets for *Les Enfants du Paradis* (uncredited, because the film was made in the Nazi period), and with whom he'd worked since *Love in the Afternoon*, to fill the Panavision screen with a similar image. Trauner designed geometric rows of desks, cheating the perspective with smaller distant lights (p. 26), smaller desks, dwarfs and even cut-outs (according to Wilder). Two years later, in his film *The Trial*, Orson Welles had his production designer Jean Mandarut produce a similar set.

Also on the set was Doane Harrison, a former Mack Sennett editor, who started working with Wilder on his first American picture as director, *The Major and the Minor*. Although Wilder had directed in Europe, he still thought of himself as a writer and came to rely on Harrison's sense of what shots would cut together and, sometimes, where the camera set-ups should be. Wilder had met

Harrison while writing for Mitchell Leisen, asked him to become his editor (on films such as *Double Indemnity, The Lost Weekend* and *Sunset Boulevard*), and finally engaged him as Associate Producer.

The cameraman was Joseph LaShelle, a 55-year-old native Californian who had won a Best Cinematography Oscar for *Laura* in 1944. This was his first Wilder picture. In the late fifties, LaShelle had worked with ex-TV directors such as Martin Ritt and Delbert Mann, so was used to the TV style of many close-ups. Wilder's wider Panavision style seems to have caused some disagreements between the two men, but LaShelle went on to shoot *Irma La Douce, Kiss Me, Stupid* and *The Fortune Cookie*, all in Panavison.

In addition to the crew and cast, for one scene (pp. 92–7) Wilder called on the advice of three doctors. When Dr Dreyfuss treats Fran after she's taken sleeping pills, the actor Jack Kruschen (who got an Oscar nomination for this role) pulls MacLaine's hair and appears to slap her hard, several times. Wilder was later criticized for the brutality of this scene, but always maintained that the set doctors advised on at least this much apparent use of force.

Shirley MacLaine's first scene in the film is the one in which she's wearing a carnation and Baxter comments on her hair (pp. 21–23). During several takes she made small adjustments to her lines. She had not been told that you do not play with Wilder's words. The director, according to Lemmon, said, 'Say the words!' 'You mean exactly?' replied MacLaine. 'Exactly!' said Wilder. 'Finally, when she did a good take,' says Lemmon, 'Billy turned to Izzy [Diamond] and Izzy whispered something to Billy and Billy said, "Let's do it just once more. You forgot the word 'and' on the second page." And he really made her do it again.'

Other accounts show that Wilder, conversely, was open to suggestions of better ways of doing things. Lemmon remembers the scene in Sheldrake's office when he has a nose spray in his hand: 'I was working out the cold scene in my dressing-room without props when suddenly I saw my hand clench on the line: 'But *I won't.*' I thought: '*This is it.*' I went to the prop department, because there's no point talking to the director, you have to try it out first. I experimented with all kinds of sprays, punching different sizes of holes in them, and finally used skim milk so the spray would show. The first time I tried it on the set, the spray went low and splurted all over the script girl. Everybody broke up. MacMurray played it exactly the way he did in the picture – just glanced at the spray, and then went on. Billy liked it so we kept it in.' Page 41 of the shooting script incorporates this visual joke in its directions, which might seem to contradict Lemmon's claim to have improvised it. If, however, he had the idea during rehearsals, it could have been incorporated into the final pre-shoot polish of the screenplay.

Another example of the actors contributing ideas comes from MacLaine. She says that Wilder used the gin rummy skills she'd learned with her friends Dean Martin, Sammy Davis and Peter Lawford in *The Apartment* screenplay. If the idea did come from MacLaine's card-playing, it must have been at quite an early writing stage, because both the scene after Fran's attempted suicide and the last one of the picture work because they use the gin rummy game as counterpoint to what is really happening, and the game is mentioned frequently in the third act of the film.

Despite the density of construction of the screenplay, there is some evidence to suggest that during the filming, Wilder wanted to make breathing spaces in the action. Lemmon remembers, for example, the early scene (p. 8) where he gets home after Kirkeby and Sylvia have been there and begins to tidy up: 'I come home and start cleaning up the place, like I'd done it every night for years before. The average director would be afraid to play it like Billy did. They'd say: "Let's get on with the scene." But Billy let that scene run two to three minutes.' Excluding Kirkeby's return visit because 'the little lady forgot her galoshes', the finished scene in the film runs nearly one and a half minutes.

To write the music for *The Apartment*, Wilder hired the 63-year-old Englishman Adolph Deutsch, who'd done the scores for the musicals *The Band Wagon, Seven Brides for Seven Brothers, Oklahoma!* and *Funny Face*, and who'd worked with Wilder before, on *Some Like it Hot*. The main theme was a tune Wilder remembered from his German days as an aficionado of American popular music. He hummed it to UA's music department, they eventually found it and Deutsch bent it this way and that to fit the ironic regretfulness of the film. The tune is identified in this screenplay as 'Jealous Lover'. Its title surprises me. Its melody certainly expresses aspects of loss and loneliness and love, but absolutely without any of the bitterness that you'd expect from jealousy.

As Kevin Lally notes, 'When it came to preview the picture, both Wilder and Diamond were nervous. Diamond agonized over reaction to the suicide scene', which was apparently his idea as a woman had committed suicide in a friend's apartment years before. Wilder 'felt that the second half of the picture was "humpbacked", with too many revelation scenes coming too close together.' They need not have worried. The preview was a great success and there was a great party afterwards at Romanoff's.

The immediate critical reception to *The Apartment* was mixed. The influential Bosley Crowther of the *New York Times* pronounced it to be 'a gleeful and sentimental film . . . kept on the side of taste and humour by the grand performance of Jack Lemmon, who takes precedence as our top comedian by virtue of this film . . . Mr Wilder's direction is ingenious and sure, tumbling with wit.' *Time* magazine was even more positive: '*The Apartment* is the funniest movie made in Hollywood since *Some Like it Hot*,' it said, '. . . [it] is a comedy of men's room humour and water-cooler politics that now and then amongst the belly laughs says something serious and sad about the struggle for success, about what it often does to a man, and about the horribly small world of big business. Director Wilder . . . holds an amazingly tight rein on actress Shirley MacLaine, which gives her performance a solidity she seldom achieves. Yet it is actor Lemmon, surely the most sensitive and tasteful young comedian now at work in Hollywood, who really cuts the mustard and carries the show.'

Not all the contemporary critics approved, however, and the nature of the disapproval became a critical orthodoxy applied regularly to Wilder's sixties films. Some said that Baxter's third act choice of love and principle over careerism and capitalist self advancement was Wilder having his cake and eating it. There would be more complaints about his perceived dismissive happy endings and false optimism (compare this film's last line 'Shut up and deal' with *Some Like it Hot's* 'Nobody's perfect' and *Kiss Me, Stupid's* 'Kiss me, stupid.')

Others thought that Wilder was cynically taking advantage of the new sixties morality and the lessening of screen censorship. Dwight Macdonald in *Esquire* said that *The Apartment* was 'immoral, that is, dishonest'. The word 'tasteless' appears regularly in the clippings and *The Saturday Review* said that the film was 'a dirty fairy tale'. The response to *Irma La Douce* (1963), *Kiss Me, Stupid* (1964) and *The Fortune Cookie* (1966) was more negative still. Where only some critics found *A Foreign Affair* (1948) and *Ace in the Hole* (1951) tasteless, a majority found the later films so.

The ambivalent critical reaction to *The Apartment* has been blurred by time. In the months that followed its release, American audiences alone saw it in such numbers that it took double its cost at the box office. Lemmon, MacLaine, Daniel Mandell, Alexander Trauner, Jack Kruschen, Wilder and Diamond were all nominated for Academy Awards that year. The film won best picture for Wilder as producer, best screenplay for Wilder and Diamond and best director for Wilder again. This was only the second time that one person had won three Oscars in one year, the first was Leo McCarey as co-writer, producer and director of *Going My Way* in 1944. The film spawned a musical, *Promises Promises*, and Wilder later said that of all his films this was the one with the fewest mistakes.

In the seventies and eighties, *The Apartment* became a favourite of television film programmers. It was cropped from its 2.35:1 Panavision shape to TV's 1.33:1, thereby losing nearly half its image. Nevertheless, its reputation continued to grow as one of the masterpieces of American cinema.

Billy Wilder tells a story of how Fritz Lang would arrive on set two hours before everybody else and make chalk marks where all the actors and camera moves should be. By the time the cast and crew turned up, everything would be planned down to the smallest detail and Lang would tolerate no changes. If you listen to the full soundtrack of *The Apartment* as you read this screenplay, you'll see that when it comes to planning, Wilder wasn't far behind. Despite his advice to write minimal scripts without detailed direction, nearly every head turn is on the page, so is virtually every word of dialogue and even much of the film grammar, such as dissolves and fades.

However, there are many small but telling differences between this, presumably the final shooting script, and the finished film. *The Apartment* starts with helicopter shots of the Manhattan skyline not, as the writers had envisaged, with Baxter's hands punching figures on a keyboard. Two and a half lines of the famous narration were cut in editing, including a bit of Jack Lemmon's character's back story, 'I started in a branch office in Cincinnati, then transferred to New York.' Towards the end, when he's telling Shirley MacLaine's Fran Kubelik that he tried to kill himself because of a girl, he says that it was in Cincinnati (pp. 135 and 136) and implies that that was his home town. Maybe there was no need to set this up earlier.

Wilder and Diamond write (p. 3) that Baxter's apartment (on 51 West 67th Street, according to Sheldrake, p. 57) 'used to be the upstairs parlour of a one-family house in the early 1900s' and that it 'has been chopped up'. Alexander Trauner's design never makes it feel like a bad conversion of a grander house, but this script note is the first hint at the theme of capitalist compartmentalized living which Wilder and Diamond seem to have wanted to explore. The screenplay specifies that Baxter had MOMA prints of Picasso, Braque and Klee (Trauner added Chagall and Rousseau, over Baxter's bed) on his walls. This seems to be one of the writers' ways of subtly humanising their insurance worker. Not a 'beatnik', as his neighbour Mrs Dreyfuss would have us believe (p. 113), but certainly someone with a bit of soul, a bit of interest in twentieth-century art. The screenplay details some of Baxter's other cultural tastes. He sings Tchaikovsky's *Italian Capriccio* (p. 139) while straining the pasta through his tennis racket, tries to take Fran to the Broadway musical *The Music Man*, is more interested in the Edmund Golding–Greta Garbo film *Grand Hotel* than westerns and listens to Dinah Shore and Perry Como. These aren't Midwestern tastes on one hand, or Greenwich Village tastes, on the other. Baxter is an urban, midtown, middlebrow man.

The biggest single scene excised in editing is on p. 6 of this screenplay. It's an exchange between Mr Kirkeby and the liveliest of the film's girlfriends, Sylvia (Joan Shawlee), in Baxter's apartment while Baxter waits outside in the rain. Sylvia says that the place is 'a real honest-to-goodness love nest' and that 'wives are getting smarter all the time'. The loss of this scene saves about forty seconds of screen time. Maybe editor Daniel Mandell and Wilder felt that the love nest point didn't need to be made. Its inclusion, especially the part about wives, would have added to the regretful, somewhat guilty and resigned times in the film when girlfriends (Kubelik, Miss Olsen) empathise with the wives of their lovers.

There are signs in the film, glimpsed moments before fade-outs, when you can see that scenes described in the screenplay were shot but not used. For example, on p. 14, Baxter was to read a copy of *Playboy* in bed, look at the centrefold and at advertisements for bowler hats, then discard the magazine and sleep. The discarding can just be seen in the film, but what preceded it is gone. It is interesting that in a script in which nearly every detail plays several roles in the weave of the story, this opportunity to explain Baxter's later purchase of the bowler hat, to emphasise his middle-management ambitions, was sacrificed. At the end of p. 13, Baxter was innocently to take a sleeping pill. This would have helped set up Kubelik's later use of the pills to attempt suicide, but it too was sacrificed in the edit.

The three cuts in Ray Walston's funny scenes with his Marilyn Monroe look-alike (pp. 15 and 19) are strange. The latter, a movie-buff joke about Maria Ouspenskaya who played the memorable fortune-teller in a couple of Wolf Man movies, is the sort of thing that might have had preview audiences scratching their heads. However the former, where Walston's Dobisch says that his girl is an ice skater 'who won't keep that long', works well on paper. Maybe the performance wasn't great, or maybe there was some problem with the closeness of the Monroe pastiche. A reference to her defacing Baxter's Picasso print with an eyebrow pencil (p. 25) was also cut.

Lemmons long office scene where he's calling colleagues to rearrange their appointments at his apartment (pp. 24–32) has four cuts in it, ranging from a few words to several exchanges. They speed up the action and improve the rhythm. The diary montages (pp. 58 and 65) suggesting nine meetings with Fran at the apartment, always on a Monday or a Thursday, also hit the cutting-room floor. Their loss robs her later, melancholic 'Monday, then Thursday, Monday again then Thursday again' of a little weight, but the style of these sequences may have seemed dated, like a throwback to a film of the thirties.

There are three other changes worth mentioning. On p. 150 of the script, after Baxter has been made Sheldrake's assistant, he sits down in his new executive washroom, takes off the sunglasses that have been hiding his black eyes and suddenly snaps them in two. Wilder and Diamond note that he is 'surprised by his own violence'. This edgy moment doesn't appear in the film. Maybe it was considered too explicit, too imprecise. It was certainly shot, however, because the breaking of the glasses action can still be glimpsed in the last few frames of the dissolve.

Towards the end of the screenplay, during a New Year's Eve party at the Chinese restaurant, Fran realizes that Baxter loves her. There is a dissolve. Wilder and Diamond write that Fran '*comes* down the street *almost* at a run'. In the finished film, of course, there's no *almost* about her run. It's a glorious, absolute run, the happiest in her life, among the most joyful in all cinema, one which the German director Volker Schlöndorff chose as his favourite cinematic moment. The screenplay underestimates what's needed at this point, one of the few places in Wilder's precision blueprint when his thinking was not complete.

And here's another little shock: in the last scene of the film, after Baxter asks Fran: 'What about Mr Sheldrake?', she says: 'We'll send him a fruitcake every Christmas,' which, in the world of this story, is what you do to ex-lovers. It's a great line because of the romance of 'every', but especially because of the 'we', the first time either has talked about being with the other. It allows Baxter to confess: 'I love you, Miss Kubelik . . . I absolutely adore you.' And yet, in the shooting script, Fran says: '*I'm* going to send him a fruitcake . . .' The 'we' is not there. The effect is cooler, more guarded. This is the only significant change of dialogue which seems to have been made during shooting. Those critics who find the present ending too optimistic, might regret the adjustment.

I love *The Apartment*. I *absolutely adore* it, but now, after a score of times seeing it, watching it over Chinese food, slo-moing MacLaine at the end as she runs along West 67th Street, I'm beginning to admire it less.

I express my qualms not to wipe the smile off your face as you begin to read about a film I presume you like, but to register my shock at the discovery of my misgivings of its greatness. *The Apartment* has given me more pleasure, more things to talk about, more phrases to use as I speak to people, than any other film (there's a sign on my door which says 'MENSCHES ONLY, PLEASE'). Now, I wonder if I allowed it to get too close to me.

It gets very close to people indeed. Hum the theme song of *The Apartment* and you feel the stupendous loneliness of being in New York. Played faster and with more brass and it becomes Fran's dream song as she runs at the end. Fran and Mr Sheldrake fell in love to the same tune; the pianist at the Chinese restaurant plays it when they arrive; Fran buys it for Sheldrake at Christmas. It is the song of their love as much as 'As Time Goes By' in *Casablanca*.

The Apartment gets close to people because it is *great* at the loneliness of Lemmon. Wilder and LaShelle often surround their lead actor with acres of that 2.35:1 space. The French critic Jerome Jacob said of *The Apartment*: 'In the era of Boeing, everyone has forgotten Lindbergh, everybody lives in the prison of the human face.' This, for me, is not the type of loneliness which *The Apartment* portrays. It's more like the loneliness in David Lean's *Summer Madness*: open, humane, heart-bursting. Jacob's idea is too abstract, too Kafkaesque. Baxter's loneliness isn't due to being imprisoned in some way. It is expressed when he goes to the park bench and the leaves fall, when he pretends to have a hot date in the lobby, but walks past her, when he stands alone outside *The Music Man*, when he packs alone on New Year's Eve and the camera (in one of Wilder's few non-eyelevel shots in the film) goes high, when he eats a TV dinner alone. His Picassos and Rousseaus on the wall show he has an interior life. He *is* a mensch, but isn't getting the chance to show it.

Watch *The Apartment* drunk and you don't fall asleep. Why is that? I think it's because it doesn't stop-start. It flows like a river, widening and deepening. No sub-plot peters out. And exactly because it flows, because it's a miracle of classical storytelling, it never becomes abstract. French critics have talked of its critique of conformism, its attack on consumer society. I can see what they're saying, but in doing so they're misjudging the feel of the film. Maybe if the dialogue didn't crackle, if MacLaine wasn't so beautiful, if the flow of feeling and hope and warmth wasn't so constant, I could see something abstract there. But I can't. And I don't think Wilder could. He, like so many emigrés, fell in love with those countries which *didn't* fall in love with theories. His whole cinema is about retreating from theory, from ideology, about the unfashionable observation that all human beings are the same, into humour, fate, 'so-what'ness, like the last lines of his films. Volker Schlöndorff says that this is what makes Wilder great. Wilder himself said that *The Apartment* could have been set in Hong Kong or Paris, Berlin or Rome. His targets aren't specifically America or New York, but people and those tendencies in people to take the easiest route through life, to half-live and half-think.

More and more, as time goes by, *The Apartment* seems to float free from the specifics of the dawn of the sixties, when it was released. Although some critics savaged it for seeming to herald a new contemporary immorality, it now seems to be from a 'time before' that new morality. Stand it in line with *The Graduate*, etc., and it sticks out a mile. Like other poets of the had been or never was – Orson Welles, John Ford, Pasolini – Wilder's humanism is timeless.

The great, timeless, moving humanism of the picture, however, doesn't make it a masterpiece and the reason I think it doesn't is in your hands at this moment. *The Apartment* is too much screenplay, too much soundtrack, not enough image track. It isn't a very visual film. When you watch it on a cinema screen, it is disappointing, it is almost too big. The feelings don't match the image.

There are of course some purely visual moments. Trauner's 19th floor office building set does everything Wilder wanted it to do, but it isn't Wilder's image, it's King Vidor's. The contrast between Baxter's apartment and Sheldrake's home is better, subtler, more relevant for the film. Page 101 of the screenplay calls Sheldrake's house 'split-level American', but there's far more in the imagery than this. The house is brightly lit, Wyleresque, WASPy, bourgeois, fifties, full of fake permanence and pretend content. Baxter's phone conversation with Sheldrake after Fran's suicide attempt allows Wilder to cut between the two homes. Unlike in Wyler, it's rare to come across stable families in Wilder and his portrait of the Sheldrakes – which includes them smiling on a Christmas card – is subtly visual.

Another visual moment which isn't in the script occurs when Baxter goes to Sheldrake's office the day after Karl Matuschka has punched him in the face. Baxter is wearing dark glasses to hide his black eye. When he says the word 'yeah' (top of p. 149), Wilder shoots from the side so that we can see his eyes in shadow, behind his glasses. There's no explicit dramatic point being made here, but the shot has an unusual tone and is ambiguously intimate.

Of course the story of *The Apartment* has a visual thing – Fran's cracked mirror – as a key element, and Wilder has said several times that he is proud that he was able to photograph Lemmon in the thing that makes him realize that Fran is having an affair with Sheldrake, thus bringing the love and careerism in his life into direct conflict, forcing him to choose. This is, indeed, narratively rich and satisfying, but it falls short of making meaning in purely visual terms. It is reducible to logic and words. It's writable in a screenplay.

Most of Wilder's visual ideas are equally reducible in *The Apartment*, and that is why, I think, it doesn't feel like a masterpiece. It explains itself too completely. It doesn't feel like it loves cinema, except, of course, for Fran running. If you imagine it in visual terms, the film is full of verticality, about Baxter climbing up the career ladder, Fran going up and down in the lift. And yet there's no sense of height in it. Wilder uses one of the widest, most horizontal of screen ratios, Panavision. This could have made for interesting tensions, but it doesn't.

My first ten or so viewings of *The Apartment* were on a TV screen and they've made me come to a conclusion I thought I'd never make about any film: I think it's better on TV. The film's verbal rather than visual nature, its intimacies, performances, warmth make it one of the best things you can do with your box in the corner of the room. The work of directors such as Wilder has, through repeated TV screenings of their best-known films in the last three decades, gained in critical reputation. Other, more visual, less intimate, more abstract American film-makers such as Nicholas Ray or Budd Boetticher, have been served less well by television.

I think that a film masterpiece must have images which in some way defy description. It must believe in the primacy of photography, it must leave a shape in my head. *The Apartment* doesn't do this, but it does so many other stupendous things.

It is the best non-masterpiece of American Cinema.

Mark Cousins, 1998

REFERENCES
Jerome Jacob, *Billy Wilder*, 1988
Lally, Kevin, *Wilder Times*, 1996
Prelutsky, Burt, Interview with Wilder, in *The Movies*, ed. Goldstein and Konigsberg, 1996
Turner, Adrian, Interview with Diamond in *Films and Filming*, 1982
Yeck, Joanne, *Diamond, International Dictionary of Films and Film-makers*
Zolotow, Maurice, *Billy Wilder in Hollywood*, 1988

CREDITS

The Apartment

Jack Lemmon and Billy Wilder
on the set of *The Apartment*

A DESK COMPUTER

A man's hand is punching out a series of figures on the keyboard.

BUD'S VOICE

On November first, 1959, the population of New York City
was 8,042,783. If you laid all these people end to end, figuring
an average height of five feet six and a half inches, they would
reach from Times Square to the outskirts of Karachi,
Pakistan. I know facts like this because I work for an
insurance company –

THE INSURANCE BUILDING – A WET, FALL DAY

*It's a big mother, covering a square block in lower Manhattan, all glass
and aluminum, jutting into the leaden sky.*

BUD'S VOICE

– Consolidated Life of New York. We are one of the top five
companies in the country – last year we wrote nine-point-
three billion dollars' worth of policies. Our home office has
31,259 employees – which is more than the entire population
of Natchez, Mississippi, or Gallup, New Mexico.

INT. NINETEENTH FLOOR

*Acres of gray steel desks, gray steel filing cabinets, and steel-gray faces
under indirect light. One wall is lined with glass-enclosed cubicles for the
supervisory personnel. It is all very neat, antiseptic, impersonal. The
only human touch is supplied by a bank of IBM machines, clacking
away cheerfully in the background.*

BUD'S VOICE

I work on the nineteenth floor – Ordinary Policy Department
– Premium Accounting Division – Section W – desk number
861.

DESK 861

Like every other desk, it has a small name plate attached to the side. This one reads C. C. Baxter.

Baxter is about thirty, serious, hard-working, unobtrusive. He wears a Brooks Brothers type suit, which he bought somewhere on Seventh Avenue, upstairs. There is a stack of perforated premium cards in front of him, and he is totaling them on the computing machine. He looks off.

BUD'S VOICE

My name is C. C. Baxter – C. for Calvin, C. for Clifford – however, most people call me Bud.

    I've been with Consolidated Life for three years and ten months. I started in the branch office in Cincinnati, then transferred to New York. My take-home pay is $94.70 a week, and there are the usual fringe benefits.

ELECTRIC WALL CLOCK

It shows 5:19. With a click, the minute hand jumps to 5:20, and a piercing bell goes off.

BUD'S VOICE

The hours in our department are 8:50 to 5:20 –

FULL SHOT – OFFICE

Instantly all work stops. Papers are being put away, typewriters and computing machines are covered, and everybody starts clearing out. Within ten seconds, the place is empty – except for Bud Baxter, still bent over his work, marooned in a sea of abandoned desks.

BUD'S VOICE

– they're staggered by floors, so that sixteen elevators can handle the 31,259 employees without a serious traffic jam. As for myself, I very often stay on at the office and work for an extra hour or two – especially when the weather is bad. It's not that I'm overly ambitious – it's just a way of killing time, until it's all right for me to go home. You see, I have this little problem with my apartment –

DISSOLVE TO:

STREET IN THE WEST SIXTIES – EVENING

Bud, wearing a weatherbeaten Ivy League raincoat and a narrow-brimmed brown hat, comes walking slowly down the sidewalk. He stops in front of a converted brownstone, looks up.

The windows on the second floor are lit, but the shades are drawn. From inside drifts the sound of cha-cha music.

BUD'S VOICE

I live in the West Sixties – just half a block from Central Park. My rent is $84 a month. It used to be eighty until last July when Mrs Lieberman, the landlady, put in a second-hand air conditioning unit.

  It's a real nice apartment – nothing fancy – but kind of cozy – just right for a bachelor. The only problem is – I can't always get in when I want to.

INT. THE APARTMENT – EVENING

What used to be the upstairs parlor of a one-family house in the early 1900s has been chopped up into living room, bedroom, bathroom and kitchen. The wallpaper is faded, the carpets are threadbare, and the upholstered furniture could stand shampooing. There are lots of books, a record player, stacks of records, a television set (21 inches and 24 payments), unframed prints from the Museum of Modern Art (Picasso, Braque, Klee) tacked up on the walls.

Only one lamp is lit, for mood, and a cha-cha record is spinning around on the phonograph. On the coffee table in front of the couch are a couple of cocktail glasses, a pitcher with some martini dregs, an almost empty bottle of vodka, a soup bowl with a few melting ice cubes at the bottom, some potato chips, an ashtray filled with cigar stubs and lipstick-stained cigarette butts, and a woman's handbag.

Mr Kirkeby, a dapper, middle-aged man, stands in front of the mirror above the fake fireplace, buttoning up his vest. He does not notice that the buttons are out of alignment.

KIRKEBY
(calling off)
Come on, Sylvia. It's getting late.

Sylvia, a first baseman of a dame, redheaded and saftig, comes cha-cha-ing into the room, trying to fasten a necklace as she hums along with the music. She dances amorously up to Kirkeby.

> **KIRKEBY**
> Cut it out, Sylvia. We got to get out of here.

He helps her with the necklace, then turns off the phonograph.

> **SYLVIA**
> What's the panic? I'm going to have another martooni.

She crosses to the coffee table, starts to pour the remnants of the vodka into the pitcher.

> **KIRKEBY**
> Please, Sylvia! It's a quarter to nine!

> **SYLVIA**
> (*dropping slivers of ice into the pitcher*)
> First you can't wait to get me up here, and now – rush, rush, rush! Makes a person feel cheap.

> **KIRKEBY**
> Sylvia – sweetie – it's not that – but I promised the guy I'd be out of here by eight o'clock, positively.

> **SYLVIA**
> (*pouring martini*)
> What guy? Whose apartment is this, anyway?

> **KIRKEBY**
> (*exasperated*)
> What's the difference? Some schnook that works in the office.

EXT. BROWNSTONE HOUSE – EVENING

Bud is pacing back and forth, throwing an occasional glance at the lit windows of his apartment. A middle-aged woman with a dog on a leash approaches along the sidewalk. She is Mrs Lieberman, the dog is a Scottie, and they are both wearing raincoats. Seeing them, Bud leans casually against the stoop.

MRS LIEBERMAN
Good evening, Mr Baxter.

BUD
Good evening, Mrs Lieberman.

MRS LIEBERMAN
Some weather we're having. Must be from all the meshugass
at Cape Canaveral,
> (*she is half-way up the steps*)

You locked out of your apartment?

BUD
No, no. Just waiting for a friend. Good night, Mrs
Lieberman.

MRS LIEBERMAN
Good night, Mr Baxter.

*She and the Scottie disappear into the house. Bud resumes pacing, his eyes
on the apartment windows. Suddenly he stops – the lights have gone out.*

Kirkeby, in coat and hat, stands in the open doorway of the darkened apartment.

> KIRKEBY
>
> Come on – come on, Sylvia!

Sylvia comes cha-cha-ing out, wearing an imitation Persian lamb coat, her hat askew on her head, bag, gloves, and an umbrella in her hand.

> SYLVIA
>
> Some set-up you got here. A real, honest-to-goodness love nest.

> KIRKEBY
>
> Sssssh.

He locks the door, slips the key under the doormat.

> SYLVIA
> (*still cha-cha-ing*)
> You're one button off, Mr Kirkeby.

She points to his exposed vest. Kirkeby looks down, sees that the buttons are out of line. He starts to rebutton them as they move down the narrow, dimly lit stairs.

> SYLVIA
>
> You got to watch those things. Wives are getting smarter all the time. Take Mr Bernheim – in the Claims Department – came home one night with lipstick on his shirt – told his wife he had a shrimp cocktail for lunch – so she took it out to the lab and had it analyzed – so now she has the house in Great Neck and the children and the new Jaguar –

> KIRKEBY
>
> Don't you ever stop talking?

EXT. BROWNSTONE HOUSE – EVENING

Bud, standing on the sidewalk, sees the front door start to open. He moves quickly into the areaway, almost bumping into the ash-cans,

*stands in the shadow of the stoop with his back turned discreetly toward
Kirkeby and Sylvia as they come down the steps.*

> KIRKEBY

Where do you live?

> SYLVIA

I told you – with my mother.

> KIRKEBY

Where does *she* live?

> SYLVIA

A hundred and seventy-ninth street – the Bronx.

> KIRKEBY

All right – I'll take you to the subway.

> SYLVIA

Like hell you will. You'll buy me a cab.

> KIRKEBY

Why do all you dames have to live in the Bronx?

> SYLVIA

You mean you bring other girls up here?

> KIRKEBY

Certainly not. I'm a happily married man.

*They move down the street. Bud appears from the areaway, glances
after them, then mounts the steps, goes through the front door.*

INT. VESTIBULE – EVENING

*There are eight mailboxes. Bud opens his, takes out a magazine in a
paper wrapper and a few letters, proceeds up the staircase.*

INT. SECOND FLOOR LANDING – EVENING

*Bud, glancing through his mail, comes up to the door of his apartment.
As he bends down to lift the doormat, the door of the rear apartment
opens and Mrs Dreyfuss, a jovial, well-fed, middle-aged woman, puts
out a receptacle full of old papers and empty cans. Bud looks around
from his bent position.*

9

                              BUD
Oh. Hello there, Mrs Dreyfuss.

                         MRS DREYFUSS
Something the matter?

                              BUD
I seem to have dropped my key.
                    (*faking a little search*)
Oh – here it is.

He slides it out from under the mat, straightens up.

                         MRS DREYFUSS
Such a racket I heard in your place – maybe you had burglars.

                              BUD
Oh, you don't have to worry about that – nothing in here that
anybody would want to steal . . .
                    (*unlocking door quickly*)
Good night, Mrs Dreyfuss.

He ducks into the apartment.

INT. APARTMENT – EVENING

*Bud snaps on the lights, drops the mail and the key on a small table,
looks around with distaste at the mess his visitors have left behind. He
sniffs the stale air, crosses to the window, pulls up the shade, opens it
wide. Now he takes off his hat and raincoat, gathers up the remains
of the cocktail party from the coffee table. Loaded down with glasses,
pitcher, empty vodka bottle, ice bowl, and potato chips, he starts toward
the kitchen.*

*The doorbell rings. Bud stops, undecided what to do with the stuff in his
hands, then crosses to the hall door, barely manages to get it open. Mr
Kirkeby barges in past him.*

                           KIRKEBY
The little lady forgot her galoshes.

He scours the room for the missing galoshes.

BUD

Mr Kirkeby, I don't like to complain – but you were supposed to be out of here by eight.

KIRKEBY

I know, Buddy-boy, I know. But those things don't always run on schedule – like a Greyhound bus.

BUD

I don't mind in the summer – but on a rainy night – and I haven't had any dinner yet –

KIRKEBY

Sure, sure. Look, kid – I put in a good word for you with Sheldrake, in Personnel.

BUD
(perking up)

Mr Sheldrake?

KIRKEBY

That's right. We were discussing our department – manpower-wise – and promotion-wise –
(finds the galoshes behind a chair)
– and I told him what a bright boy you were. They're always on the lookout for young executives.

BUD

Thank you, Mr Kirkeby.

KIRKEBY
(starting toward the door)

You're on your way up, Buddy-boy. And you're practically out of liquor.

BUD

I know. Mr Eichelberger – in the Mortgage Loan Department – last night he had a little Halloween party here –

KIRKEBY

Well, lay in some vodka and some vermouth – and put my name on it.

11

BUD

Yes, Mr Kirkeby. You still owe me for the last two bottles –

KIRKEBY

I'll pay you on Friday.

(*in the open doorway*)

And whatever happened to those little cheese crackers you used to have around?

He exits, shutting the door.

BUD

(*making a mental note*)

Cheese crackers.

He carries his load into the kitchen.

The kitchen is minute and cluttered. On the drainboard are an empty vermouth bottle, some ice-cube trays, a jar with one olive in it, and a crumpled potato-chip bag.

Bud comes in, dumps his load on the drainboard, opens the old-fashioned refrigerator. He takes out a frozen chicken dinner, turns the oven on, lights it with a match, rips the protective paper off the aluminum tray and shoves it in.

Now he starts to clean up the mess on the drainboard. He rinses the cocktail glasses, is about to empty the martini pitcher into the sink, thinks better of it. He pours the contents into a glass, plops the lone olive out of the jar, scoops up the last handful of potato chips, toasts an imaginary companion, and drinks up. Then he pulls a wastebasket from under the sink. It is brimful of liquor bottles, and Bud adds the empty vodka and vermouth bottles and the olive jar. Picking up the heavy receptacle, he carries it through the living room toward the hall door.

INT. SECOND FLOOR LANDING – EVENING

The door of Bud's apartment opens, and Bud comes out with the wastebasket full of empty bottles. Just then, Dr David Dreyfuss, whose wife we met earlier, comes trudging up the stairs. He is a tall, heavy-set man of fifty, with a bushy mustache, wearing a bulky overcoat and carrying an aged medical bag.

DR DREYFUSS

Good evening, Baxter.

BUD

Hi, Doc. Had a late call?

DR DREYFUSS

Yeah. Some clown at Schrafft's 57th Street ate a club sandwich, and forgot to take out the toothpick.

BUD

Oh.
(*sets down wastebasket*)
'Bye, Doc.

DR DREYFUSS
(*indicating bottles*)

Say, Baxter – the way you're belting that stuff, you must have a pair of cast-iron kidneys.

BUD

Oh, that's not me. It's just that once in a while, I have some people in for a drink.

DR DREYFUSS

As a matter of fact, you must be an iron man all around. From what I hear through the walls, you got something going for you every night.

BUD

I'm sorry if it gets noisy –

DR DREYFUSS

Sometimes, there's a twi-night double-header.
(*shaking his head*)
A nebbish like you!

BUD
(*uncomfortable*)

Yeah. Well – see you, Doc.
(*starts to back through door*)

DR DREYFUSS

You know, Baxter – I'm doing some research at the

Columbia Medical Center – and I wonder if you could do us a favor?

BUD

Me?

DR DREYFUSS

When you make out your will – and the way you're going, you should – would you mind leaving your body to the University?

BUD

My body? I'm afraid you guys would be disappointed. Good night, Doc.

DR DREYFUSS

Slow down, kid.

He starts into the rear apartment as Bud closes the door.

INT. APARTMENT – EVENING

Bud, loosening his tie, goes into the kitchen, opens the oven, turns off the gas. He takes a Coke out of the refrigerator, uncaps it, gets a knife and fork from a drawer, and using his handkerchief as a potholder, pulls the hot aluminum tray out of the oven. He carries everything out into the living room.

In the living room, Bud sets his dinner down on the coffee table, settles himself on the couch. He rears up as something stabs him, reaches under his buttocks, pulls out a hairpin. He drops it into an ashtray, tackles his dinner. Without even looking, he reaches over to the end table and presses the remote TV station-selector. He takes a sip from the Coke bottle, his eyes on the TV screen across the room.

The picture on the TV set jells quickly. Against a background of criss-crossing searchlights, a pompous announcer is making his spiel.

ANNOUNCER

– from the world's greatest library of film classics, we proudly present –

(fanfare)

Greta Garbo – John Barrymore – Joan Crawford – Wallace Beery – and Lionel Barrymore in –

14

(fanfare)

Grand Hotel!

There is an extended fanfare. Bud leans forward, chewing excitedly on a chicken leg.

But first, a word from our sponsor. If you smoke the modern way, don't be fooled by phony filter claims –

Bud still eating, automatically reaches for the station-selector, pushes the button.

A new channel pops on. It features a Western – cockamamie Indians are attacking a stagecoach.

That's not for Bud. He switches to another station. In a frontier saloon, Gower Street cowboys are dismantling the furniture and each other.

Bud wearily changes channels. But he can't get away from Westerns – on this station, the US Cavalry is riding to the rescue. Will they get there in time?

Bud doesn't wait to find out. He switches channels again, and is back where he started.

On the screen, once more, is the announcer standing in front of the criss-crossing searchlights.

And now, *Grand Hotel* – starring Greta Garbo, John Barrymore, Joan Crawford –

Bud is all eyes and ears again.

– Wallace Beery, and Lionel Barrymore. But first – a word from our *alternate* sponsor.
(unctuously)
Friends, do you have wobbly dentures – ?

That does it. Bud turns the set off in disgust.

The TV screen blacks out, except for a small pinpoint of light in the center, which gradually fades away.

In the bathroom, Bud, in pajamas by now, is brushing his teeth. From his shower rod hang three pairs of socks on stretchers. Bud takes a vial from the medicine shelf, shakes out a sleeping pill, washes it down

15

with a glass of water. He turns the light off, walks into the bedroom.

In the bedroom, the single bed is made, and the lamp on the night table is on. Bud plugs in the electric blanket, turns the dial on. Then he climbs into bed, props up the pillow behind him. From the night table, he picks up the magazine that arrived in the mail, slides it out of the wrapper, opens it. It's the new issue of Playboy. *Bud leafs through it till he comes to the* pièce de resistance *of the magazine. He unfolds the overleaf, glances at it casually, refolds it, then turns to the back of the magazine and starts to read.*

What he is so avidly interested in is the men's fashion section. There is a layout titled 'What The Young Executive Will Wear', with a sub-head reading 'The Bowler is Back'. Illustrating the article are several photographs of male models wearing various styles of bowlers.

Bud is definitely in the market for a bowler, but somehow his mind starts wandering. He turns back to the overleaf again, unfolds it, studies it, then holds the magazine up vertically to get a different perspective on the subject. By now the sleeping pill is beginning to take effect, and he yawns. He drops the magazine on the floor, kills the light, settles down to sleep. The room is dark except for the glow from the dial of the electric blanket.

Three seconds. Then the phone jangles shrilly in the living room. Bud stumbles groggily out of bed, and putting on his slippers, makes his way into the living room. He switches on the light, picks up the phone.

BUD

Hello? – Hello? – yes, this is Baxter.

INT. PHONE BOOTH IN A MANHATTAN BAR – NIGHT

On the phone is a hearty man of about forty-five, nothing but personality, most of it obnoxious. His name is Dobisch. Outside the booth is a blonde babe, slightly boozed, and beyond there is a suggestion of the packed, smoky joint.

DOBISCH

Hiya, Buddy-boy. I'm in this bar on Sixty-first Street – and I got to thinking about you – and I figured I'd give you a little buzz.

16

BUD – ON PHONE

>   **BUD**
> Well, that's very nice of you – but who is this?

INT. PHONE BOOTH

>   **DOBISCH**
> Dobisch – Joe Dobisch, in Administration.

BUD – ON PHONE

>   **BUD**
>   (*snapping to attention*)
> Oh, yes, Mr Dobisch. I didn't recognize your voice –

INT. PHONE BOOTH

>   **DOBISCH**
> That's okay, Buddy-boy. Now like I was saying, I'm in this
> joint on Sixty-first – and I think I got lucky –
>   (*glances toward blonde*)
> – she's a skater with the Ice Show –
>   (*he chuckles*)
> – and I thought maybe I could bring her up for a quiet drink.

BUD – ON PHONE

>   **BUD**
> I'm sorry, Mr Dobisch. You know I like to help you guys out
> – but it's sort of late – so why don't we make it some other
> time?

INT. PHONE BOOTH

>   **DOBISCH**
> Buddy-boy – she won't keep that long – not even on ice.
> Listen, kid, I can't pass this up – she looks like Marilyn
> Monroe.

> ### BUD
> I don't care if it *is* Marilyn Monroe – I'm already in bed – and I've taken a sleeping pill – so I'm afraid the answer is no.

INT. PHONE BOOTH

> ### DOBISCH
> (*pulling rank*)
> Look, Baxter – we're making out the monthly efficiency rating – and I'm putting you in the top ten. Now you don't want to louse yourself up, do you?

BUD – ON PHONE

> ### BUD
> Of course not. But – how can I be efficient in the office if I don't get enough sleep at night?

INT. PHONE BOOTH

> ### DOBISCH
> It's only eleven – and I just want the place for forty-five minutes.

The blonde opens the door of the phone booth, leans in.

> ### BLONDE
> I'm getting lonely. Who are you talking to, anyway?

> ### DOBISCH
> My mother.

> ### BLONDE
> That's sweet. That's real sweet.

Dobisch shuts the door in her face.

> ### DOBISCH
> (*into phone again*)
> Make it thirty minutes. What do you say, Bud?

INT. APARTMENT

BUD
(*a last stand*)
I'm all out of liquor – and there's no clean glasses – no cheese crackers – no nothing.

INT. PHONE BOOTH

DOBISCH
Let me worry about that. Just leave the key under the mat and clear out.

INT. APARTMENT

BUD
(*into phone; resigned*)
Yes, Mr Dobisch.

He hangs up, shuffles back into the bedroom.

(*muttering to himself*)
Anything you say, Mr Dobisch – no trouble at all, Mr Dobisch – be my guest –

He reappears from the bedroom, pulling his trousers on over his pajama pants.

– We never close at Buddy-boy's – looks like Marilyn Monroe –

He chuckles à la Dobisch.

Putting on his raincoat and hat, Bud opens the hall door, takes the key from the table, shoves it under the doormat. His eyes fall on the Dreyfuss apartment, and there is some concern on his face. He picks up a pad and pencil from the table, prints something in block letters. Tearing off the top sheet, he impales it on the spindle of the phonograph, then walks out, closing the door behind him. The note reads:

NOT TOO LOUD
THE NEIGHBORS ARE COMPLAINING

19

EXT. BROWNSTONE HOUSE – NIGHT

Bud comes out the door, in slippered feet, pants and raincoat over his pajamas. As he sleep-walks down the steps, a cab pulls up in front of the house. Bud ducks discreetly into the areaway.

Mr Dobisch, bare-headed, emerges cautiously from the cab. Between the fingers of his hands he is carrying four long-stemmed glasses, brimful of stingers. The blonde steps out, holding his hat.

> BLONDE

This the place?

> DOBISCH

Yeah.
> (*to cab driver*)

How much?

> CABBIE

Seventy cents.

Dobisch, his hands full of stingers, turns to the blonde, indicates his pants pocket.

> DOBISCH

Get the money, will you?

The blonde plants the hat on top of his head, unbuttons his overcoat, reaches into his pants pocket. As she does so, she jogs his elbow.

Watch those stingers!

The blonde has taken out Dobisch's money clip, with about a hundred dollars in it.

Give him a buck.

The blonde peels a bill off, hands it to the cabbie, hangs on to the rest of the roll just a second too long.

Now put it back honey.
> (*she does*)

Atta girl.

The cab drives off. Dobisch and the blonde start up the steps to the house.

BLONDE

You sure this is a good idea?

DOBISCH

Can't think of a better one.

BLONDE
(*holding door open for him*)
I mean – barging in on your mother – in the middle of the night?

DOBISCH
(*edging past her with stingers*)
Don't worry about the old lady. One squawk from her, and she's out of a job.

In the areaway, Bud has overheard them, and it doesn't make him any happier. He steps out on the sidewalk, shuffles down the street.

INT. SECOND FLOOR LANDING – NIGHT

The blonde and Dobisch, his hands full of stingers, come up to Bud's door.

DOBISCH

Get the key, will you.

Automatically, she reaches into his pocket.

Not there. Under the mat.

BLONDE
(*puzzled*)

Under the mat?

(*picks up key*)

DOBISCH
(*impatiently*)
Open up, open up – we haven't got all night.

The blonde unlocks the door to the apartment, opens it.

BLONDE
(*suspiciously*)
So this is your mother's apartment?

That's right. Maria Ouspenskaya.

BLONDE
(*sticking her head in*)
Hiya, Ouspenskaya.

Dobisch nudges her inside with his knee, follows, kicks the door shut behind him.

The landing is empty for a second. Then the door of the rear apartment opens, and Dr Dreyfuss, in a beaten bathrobe, sets out a couple of empty milk bottles with a note in them. Suddenly, from Bud's apartment, comes a shrill female giggle. Dr Dreyfuss reacts. Then the cha-cha music starts full blast.

DR DREYFUSS
(*calling to his wife; off-scene*)
Mildred – he's at it again.

Shaking his head, he closes the door.

EXT. CENTRAL PARK – NIGHT

Bud, in raincoat and slippered feet, turns in off the street, plods along a path in the deserted park. He stops at a damp bench under a lamp post, sits. In the background, lights shine from the towering buildings on Central Park South.

Bud huddles inside his raincoat, shivering. He is very sleepy by now. His eyes close and his head droops. A gust of wind sends wet leaves swirling across the bench. Bud doesn't stir. He is all in.

FADE OUT:

FADE IN:

INT. LOBBY INSURANCE BUILDING – DAY

It's a quarter to nine of a gray November morning, and work-bound employees are piling in through the doors. Among them is Bud, bundled up in a raincoat, hat, heavy muffler and wool gloves, and carrying a box of Kleenex. He coughs, pulls out a tissue, wipes his dripping nose. He has a bad cold.

The lobby is an imposing, marbled affair, as befits a company which last year wrote 9.3 billion dollars' worth of insurance. There are sixteen elevators, eight of them marked LOCAL – FLOORS 1–18, and opposite them marked express – FLOORS 18–37. The starter, a uniformed Valkyrie wielding a clicker, is directing the flow of traffic into the various elevators.

Bud joins the crowd in front of one of the express elevators. Also standing there is Mr Kirkeby, reading the Herald-Tribune.

BUD

(hoarsely)

Good morning, Mr Kirkeby

KIRKEBY

(as if he just knew him vaguely)

Oh, how are you, Baxter. They keeping you busy these days?

BUD

Yes, sir. They are indeed.

(he sniffs)

The elevator doors open, revealing the operator. She is in her middle twenties and her name is Fran Kubelik. Maybe it's the way she's put together, maybe it's her face, or maybe it's just the uniform – in any case, there is something very appealing about her. She is also an individualist – she wears a carnation in her lapel, which is strictly against regulations. As the elevator loads, she greets the passengers cheerfully.

FRAN

(rattling it off)

Morning, Mr Kessel – Morning, Miss Robinson – Morning, Mr Kirkeby – Morning, Mr Williams – Morning, Miss Livingston – Morning, Mr McKellway – Morning, Mr Pirelli – Morning, Mrs Schubert –

Interspersed is an occasional 'Morning, Miss Kubelik' from the passengers.

Morning, Mr Baxter.

BUD

Morning, Miss Kubelik.

23

He takes his hat off – he is the only one. The express is now loaded.

> STARTER
> (*working the clicker*)
> That's all. Take it away.

> FRAN
> (*shutting the door*)
> Watch the door, please. Blasting off.

INT. ELEVATOR

Bud is standing right next to Fran as the packed express shoots up.

> BUD
> (*studying her*)
> What did you do to your hair?

> FRAN
> It was making me nervous, so I chopped it off. Big mistake, huh?

> BUD
> I sort of like it.

He sniffs, takes out a Kleenex, wipes his nose.

> FRAN
> Say, you got a lulu.

> BUD
> Yeah. I better not get too close.

> FRAN
> Oh, I never catch colds.

> BUD
> Really? I was looking at some figures from the Sickness and Accident Claims Division – do you know that the average New Yorker between the ages of twenty and fifty has two and a half colds a year?

> FRAN
> That makes me feel just terrible.

                         BUD
Why?

                        FRAN
Well, to make the figures come out even – since I have *no*
colds a year – some poor slob must have *five* colds a year.

                         BUD
That's me.
                    (*dabs his nose*)

                        FRAN
You should have stayed in bed this morning.

                         BUD
I should have stayed in bed last night.

The elevator has slowed down, now stops. Fran opens the door.

                        FRAN
Nineteen. Watch your step.

*About a third of the passengers get out, including Bud and Mr Kirkeby.
As Kirkeby passes Fran, he slaps her behind with his folded newspaper.
Fran jumps slightly – all in a day's work.*

And watch your hand, Mr Kirkeby!

                      KIRKEBY
                    (*innocently*)
I beg your pardon?

                        FRAN
One of these days I'm going to shut those doors on you and –

*She withdraws her hand into the sleeve of her uniform, and waves the
'amputated' arm at him.*

Twenty next.

The doors close.

INT. NINETEENTH FLOOR – DAY

*Kirkeby turns away from the elevator, and grinning smugly, falls in
beside Bud.*

KIRKEBY

That Kubelik – boy! Would I like to get her on a slow elevator to China.

BUD

Oh, yes. She's the best operator in the building.

KIRKEBY

I'm a pretty good operator myself – but she just won't give me a tumble – date-wise.

BUD

Maybe you're using the wrong approach.

KIRKEBY

A lot of guys around here have tried it – all kinds of approaches – no dice. What is she trying to prove?

BUD

Could be she's just a nice, respectable girl – there are millions of them.

KIRKEBY

Listen to him. Little Lord Fauntleroy!

Leaving Bud at the employees' coat-racks, Kirkeby heads toward his office, one of the glass-enclosed cubicles. Bud hangs up his hat and raincoat, stows away the gloves and muffler. Out of his coat pocket he takes a plastic anti-histamine sprayer and a box of cough drops, and still carrying the Kleenex, threads his way to his desk. Most of the desks are already occupied, and the others are filling rapidly.

Once seated at his desk, Bud arranges his medicaments neatly in front of him. He takes a Kleenex out of the box, blows his nose, then leaning back in his swivel chair sprays first one nostril, then the other. Suddenly the piercing bell goes off – the workday has begun. Being the ultra-conscientious type, Bud instantly sits upright in his chair, removes the cover from his computing machine, picks up a batch of perforated premium cards, starts entering figures on his computer.

After a few seconds, he glances around to make sure that everybody in the vicinity is busy. Then he looks up a number in the company telephone directory, dials furtively.

BUD
(*cupping hand over phone mouthpiece*)
Hello, Mr Dobisch? This is Baxter, on the nineteenth floor.

INT. DOBISCH'S OFFICE – DAY

It is a glass-enclosed cubicle on the twenty-first floor. Through the glass we see another enormous layout of desks, everybody working away. Dobisch is holding the phone in one hand, running an electric shaver over his face with the other.

DOBISCH
Oh, Buddy-boy. I was just about to call you.
(*shuts off electric shaver*)
I'm sorry about that mess on the living room wall. You see, my little friend, she kept insisting Picasso was a bum – so she started to do that mural – but I'm sure it will wash off – just eyebrow pencil.

BUD – ON PHONE

BUD
It's not Picasso I'm calling about. It's the key – to my apartment – you were supposed to leave it under the mat.

DOBISCH – ON PHONE

DOBISCH
I did, didn't I? I distinctly remember bending over and putting it there –

BUD – ON PHONE

BUD
Oh, I found a key there, all right – only it's the wrong key.

DOBISCH – ON PHONE

DOBISCH
It is?

(takes Bud's key out of his pocket)
Well, how about that? No wonder I couldn't get into the
executive washroom this morning.

BUD – ON PHONE

> BUD
>
> And I couldn't get into my apartment – so at four a.m. I
> had to wake up the landlady and give her a whole song and
> dance about going out to mail a letter and the door
> slamming shut.

DOBISCH – ON PHONE

> DOBISCH
>
> That's a shame. I'll send the key right down. And about your
> promotion –
> *(leafs through report on desk)*
> – I'm sending that efficiency report right up to Mr Sheldrake,
> in Personnel. I wouldn't be surprised if you heard from him
> before the day is over.

BUD – ON PHONE

> BUD
>
> Thank you, Mr Dobisch.

*He hangs up, feels his forehead. It is warm. Clipped to his handkerchief
pocket are a black fountain pen and, next to it, a thermometer in a
black case. Bud unclips the thermometer case, unscrews the cap, shakes
the thermometer out, puts it under his tongue. He resumes work.*

A messenger comes up to his desk with an inter-office envelope.

> MESSENGER
>
> From Mr Dobisch.

> BUD
> *(thermometer in mouth)*
>
> Wait.

*He turns away from the messenger, unties the string of the envelope,
takes his key out, puts it in a coat pocket. From a trouser pocket, he*

*extracts Dobisch's key to the executive washroom, slips it discreetly into
the envelope, reties it, hands it to the messenger.*

> BUD
> (*thermometer in mouth*)
>
> *To* Mr Dobisch.

*Puzzled by the whole procedure, the messenger leaves. Bud now removes
the thermometer from his mouth, reads it. It's worse than he thought.
He puts the thermometer back in the case, clips it to his pocket, takes
his desk calender out of a drawer, turns a leaf. Under the date*
WEDNESDAY, NOVEMBER 4 *there is an entry in his handwriting – Mr
Vanderhof. Bud consults the telephone directory again, he picks up the
phone, dials.*

INT. VANDERHOF'S OFFICE – DAY

*This is another glass-enclosed cubicle on another floor. Mr Vanderhof, a
Junior Chamber of Commerce type, is dictating to an elderly secretary
who sits across the desk from him.*

> VANDERHOF
>
> Dear Mr MacIntosh –
> (*phone rings and he picks it up*)
> Vanderhof, Public Relations. Oh, yes, Baxter. Just a minute.
> (*to secretary*)
> All right, Miss Finch – type up what we got so far.

He waits till she is out of the office; then, into phone:

> Now, what is it, Baxter?

BUD – ON PHONE

> BUD
>
> Look, Mr Vanderhof – I've got you down here for tonight –
> but I'm going to be using the place myself – so I'll have to
> cancel.

VANDERHOF – ON PHONE

> VANDERHOF
>
> Cancel? But it's her birthday – I already ordered the cake –

30

BUD – ON PHONE

BUD

I hate to disappoint you – I mean, many happy returns – but
not tonight –

VANDERHOF – ON PHONE

VANDERHOF

That's not like you, Baxter. Just the other day, at the staff
meeting, I was telling Mr Sheldrake what a reliable man you
were.

BUD – ON PHONE

BUD

Thank you, Mr Vanderhof. But I'm sick – I have this terrible
cold – and a fever – and I got to go to bed right after work.

VANDERHOF – ON PHONE

VANDERHOF

Buddy-boy, that's the worst thing you can do. If you get a
cold, you should go to a Turkish bath – spend the night there
– sweat it out –

BUD – ON PHONE

BUD

Oh, no. I'd get pneumonia – and if I got pneumonia, I'd be in
bed for a month – and if I were in bed for a month –

VANDERHOF – ON PHONE

VANDERHOF

Okay, you made your point. We'll just have to do it *next*
Wednesday – that's the only night of the week I can get away.

BUD – ON PHONE

BUD

Wednesday – Wednesday –

(leafing through calendar)
I got somebody pencilled in – let me see what I can do – I'll
get back to you.

*He hangs up, rifles through the directory, finds the number, and with a
furtive look around, dials again.*

BUD
(into phone)
Mr Eichelberger? Is this Mortgage and Loan? I'd like to speak
to Mr Eichelberger. Yes, it *is* urgent.

INT. EICHELBERGER'S OFFICE – DAY

*Also glass-enclosed, but slightly larger than the others. Mr Eichelberger,
a solid citizen of about fifty, is displaying some mortgage graphs to three
associates. A fourth one has answered the phone.*

ASSOCIATE
(holding out phone to Eichelberger)
For you, Mel.

Eichelberger puts the charts down, takes the phone.

EICHELBERGER
Eichelberger here – oh, yes, Baxter –

*A glance at his associates; then continues, as though it were a business
call.*

What's your problem? – Wednesday is out? – Oh – that
throws a little monkey wrench into my agenda – Thursday?
No, I'm all tied up on Thursday – let's schedule that meeting
for Friday.

BUD – ON PHONE

BUD
Friday?
(checks calender)
Let me see what I can do. I'll get back to you.

He hangs up, consults the directory, starts to dial a number.

INT. KIRKEBY'S OFFICE – DAY

It's another of those glass-enclosed cubicles, on the nineteenth floor. Kirkeby is talking into a dictaphone.

                    KIRKEBY
Premium-wise and billing-wise, we are eighteen percent ahead of last year, October-wise.

The phone has been ringing. Kirkeby switches off the machine, picks up the phone.

Hello? Yeah, Baxter. What's up?

BUD – ON PHONE

                    BUD
Instead of Friday – could you possibly switch to Thursday? You'd be doing me a great favor –

KIRKEBY – ON PHONE

                    KIRKEBY
Well – it's all right with *me*, Bud. Let me check. I'll get back to you.

He presses down the button on the cradle, dials Operator.

INT. SWITCHBOARD ROOM

There is a double switchboard in the center, with nine girls on each side, all busy as beavers. In the foreground we recognize Sylvia, Kirkeby's date of last night.

                    SYLVIA
Consolidated Life – I'll connect you – Consolidated Life –

The girl next to her turns and holds out a line.

                    SWITCHBOARD GIRL
Sylvia – it's for you.

Sylvia plugs the call into her own switchboard.

SYLVIA

Yes? Oh, hello – sure I got home all right – you owe me forty-five cents.

KIRKEBY – ON PHONE

KIRKEBY

Okay, okay. Look, Sylvia – instead of Friday – could we make it Thursday night?

SYLVIA – AT SWITCHBOARD

SYLVIA

Thursday? That's *The Untouchables.* – with Bob Stack.

KIRKEBY – ON PHONE

KIRKEBY

Bob *who?* – all right, so we'll watch it at the apartment. Big deal.
               (he hangs up, dials)
Baxter? It's okay for Thursday.

INT. NINETEENTH FLOOR – DAY

Bud, at his desk, is on the phone.

BUD

Thank you, Mr Kirkeby.
               (hangs up, consults directory, dials)
Mr Eichelberger? It's okay for Friday.
               (hangs up, consults directory, dials)
Mr Vanderhof? It's okay for Wednesday.

During this, the phone has rung at the next desk, and the occupant, Mr Moffett, has picked it up. As Bud hangs up –

MOFFETT
(into phone)
All right – I'll tell him.
               (hangs up, turns to Bud)
Hey, Baxter – that was Personnel.
Mr Sheldrake's secretary.

                              BUD
Sheldrake?

                            MOFFETT
She's been trying to reach you for the last twenty minutes.
They want you upstairs.

                              BUD
Oh!

*He jumps up, stuffs the nose-spray into one pocket, a handful of Kleenex
into the other.*

                            MOFFETT
What gives, Baxter? You getting promoted or getting fired?

                              BUD
                            (*cockily*)
Care to make a small wager?

                            MOFFETT
I've been here twice as long as you have –

                              BUD
Shall we say – a dollar?

                            MOFFETT
It's a bet.

Bud snake-hips between the desks like a broken-field runner.

*At the elevator, Bud presses the up button, paces nervously. One of the
elevator doors opens, and as Bud starts inside, the doors of the adjoining
elevator open, and Fran Kubelik sticks her head out.*

                             FRAN
Going up?

*Hearing her voice, Bud throws a quick 'Excuse me' to the other
operator, exits quickly and steps into Fran's elevator.*

                              BUD
Twenty-seven, please. And drive carefully. You're carrying
precious cargo – I mean, manpower-wise.

Fran shuts the doors.

INT. ELEVATOR – DAY

Fran presses a button, and the elevator starts up.

> FRAN

Twenty-seven.

> BUD

You may not realize it, Miss Kubelik, but I'm in the top ten –
efficiency-wise – and this may be the day – promotion-wise.

> FRAN

You're beginning to sound like Mr Kirkeby already.

> BUD

Why not? Now that they're kicking me upstairs –

> FRAN

Couldn't happen to a nicer guy.

Bud beams.

You know, you're the only one around here who ever takes
his hat off in the elevator.

> BUD

Really?

> FRAN

The characters you meet. Something happens to men in
elevators. Must be the change of altitude – the blood rushes
to their head, or something – boy, I could tell you stories –

> BUD

I'd love to hear them. Maybe we could have lunch in the
cafeteria sometime – or some evening, after work –

The elevator has stopped, and Fran opens the doors.

> FRAN

Twenty-seven.

INT. TWENTY-SEVENTH FLOOR FOYER – DAY

*It is pretty plush up here – soft carpeting and tall mahogany doors leading
to the executive offices. The elevator door is open, and Bud steps out.*

FRAN

I hope everything goes all right.

BUD

I hope so.
              (*turning back*)
Wouldn't you know they'd call me on a day like this – with
my cold and everything –
              (*fumbling with his tie*)
How do I look?

FRAN

Fine.
              (*stepping out of elevator*)
Wait.

She takes the carnation out of her lapel, starts to put it in Bud's buttonhole.

BUD

Thank you. That's the first thing I ever noticed about you –
when you were still on the local elevator – you always wore a
flower –

The elevator buzzer is now sounding insistently. Fran steps back inside.

FRAN

Good luck. And wipe your nose.

*She shuts the doors. Bud looks after her, then takes a Kleenex out of his
pocket, and wiping his nose, crosses to a glass door marked J. D.
SHELDRAKE, DIRECTOR OF PERSONNEL. He stashes the used Kleenex
away in another pocket, enters.*

INT. SHELDRAKE'S ANTEROOM – DAY

*It is a sedate office with a secretary and a couple of typists. The
secretary's name is Miss Olsen. She is in her thirties, flaxen-haired,
handsome, wears harlequin glasses, and has an incisive manner. Bud
comes up to her desk.*

BUD

C. C. Baxter – Ordinary Premium Accounting – Mr
Sheldrake called me.

MISS OLSEN

I called you – that is, I *tried* to call you – for twenty minutes.

BUD

I'm sorry, I –

MISS OLSEN

Go on in.

She indicates the door leading to the inner office. Bud squares his shoulders and starts in.

INT. SHELDRAKE'S OFFICE – DAY

Mr Sheldrake is a $14,000 a year man, and rates a four-window office.

It is not quite an executive suite, but it is several pegs above the glass cubicles of the middle echelon. There is lots of leather, and a large desk behind which sits Mr Sheldrake. He is a substantial looking, authoritative man in his middle forties, a pillar of his suburban community, a blood donor and a family man. The latter is attested to by a framed photograph showing two boys, aged eight and ten, in military school uniforms.

As Baxter comes through the door, Sheldrake is leafing through Dobisch's efficiency report. He looks up at Bud through a pair of heavy-rimmed reading glasses.

SHELDRAKE

Baxter?

BUD

Yes, sir.

SHELDRAKE
(*studying him*)
I was sort of wondering what you looked like. Sit down.

BUD

Yes, Mr Sheldrake.

He seats himself on the very edge of the leather armchair facing Sheldrake.

39

SHELDRAKE

Been hearing some very nice things about you – here's a
report from Mr Dobisch – loyal, cooperative, resourceful –

BUD

Mr Dobisch said that?

SHELDRAKE

And Mr Kirkeby tells me that several nights a week you work
late at the office – without overtime.

BUD
(*modestly*)
Well, you know how it is – things pile up.

SHELDRAKE

Mr Vanderhof, in Public Relations, and Mr Eichelberger, in
Mortgage and Loan – they'd both like to have you transferred
to their departments.

BUD

That's very flattering.

*Sheldrake puts the report down, takes off his glasses, leans across the
desk toward Bud.*

SHELDRAKE

Tell me, Baxter – just what is it that makes you so popular?

BUD

I don't know.

SHELDRAKE

Think.

*Bud does so. For a moment, he is a picture of intense concentration.
Then –*

BUD

Would you mind repeating the question?

SHELDRAKE

Look, Baxter, I'm not stupid. I know everything that goes on
in this building – in every department – on every floor – every
day of the year.

BUD
(*in a very small voice*)

You do?

SHELDRAKE
(*rises, starts pacing*)

In 1957, we had an employee here, name of Fowler. *He* was very popular, too. Turned out he was running a bookie joint right in the Actuarial Department – tying up the switchboard, figuring the odds on our IBM machines – so the day before the Kentucky Derby, I called in the Vice Squad and we raided the thirteenth floor.

BUD
(*worried*)

The Vice Squad?

SHELDRAKE

That's right, Baxter.

BUD

What – what's that got to do with me? I'm not running any bookie joint.

SHELDRAKE

What kind of joint *are* you running?

BUD

Sir?

SHELDRAKE

There's a certain key floating around the office – from Kirkeby to Vanderhof to Eichelberger to Dobisch – it's the key to a certain apartment – and you know who that apartment belongs to?

BUD

Who?

SHELDRAKE

Loyal, cooperative, resourceful C. C. Baxter.

BUD

Oh.

SHELDRAKE

Are you going to deny it?

BUD

No, sir. I'm not going to deny it. But if you'd just let me explain –

SHELDRAKE

You better.

BUD

(*a deep breath*)

Well, about six months ago – I was going to night school, taking this course in Advanced Accounting – and one of the guys in our department – he lives in Jersey – he was going to a banquet at the Biltmore – and his wife was meeting him in town, and he needed someplace to change into a tuxedo – so I gave him the key – and word must have gotten around – because the next thing I knew, all sorts of guys were suddenly going to banquets – and when you give the key to one guy, you can't say no to another – and the whole thing got out of hand – pardon me.

He whips out the nasal-spray, administers a couple of quick squirts up each nostril.

SHELDRAKE

Baxter, an insurance company is founded on public trust. Any employee who conducts himself in a manner unbecoming –

(*shifting into a new gear*)

How many charter members are there in this little club of yours?

BUD

Just those four – out of a total of 31,259 – so actually, we can be very proud of our personnel – percentage-wise.

SHELDRAKE

That's not the point. Four rotten apples in a barrel – no matter how large the barrel – you realize that if this ever leaked out –

BUD

Oh, it won't. Believe me. And it's not going to happen again. From now on, nobody is going to use my apartment –

In his vehemence he squeezes the spray bottle, which squirts all over the desk.

SHELDRAKE

Where *is* your apartment?

BUD

West 67th Street. You have no idea what I've been going through – with the neighbors and the landlady and the liquor and the key –

SHELDRAKE

How do you work it with the key?

BUD

Well, usually I slip it to them in the office and they leave it under the mat – but never again – I can promise you that –

The phone buzzer sounds, and Sheldrake picks up the phone.

SHELDRAKE

Yes, Miss Olsen.

INT. SHELDRAKE'S ANTEROOM – DAY

Miss Olsen is on the phone.

MISS OLSEN

Mrs Sheldrake returning your call – on two –

She presses a button down, starts to hang the phone up, glances around to see if the typists are watching, then raises the receiver to her ear and eavesdrops on the conversation.

INT. SHELDRAKE'S OFFICE – DAY

Sheldrake is talking into the phone.

SHELDRAKE

Yes, dear – I called you earlier – where were you? Oh, you took Tommy to the dentist –

During this, Bud has risen from his chair, started inching toward the door.

                    SHELDRAKE
                  (*turning to him*)
Where are you going, Baxter?

                    BUD
Well, I don't want to intrude – and I thought – since it's all
straightened out anyway –

                    SHELDRAKE
I'm not through with you yet.

                    BUD
Yes, sir.

                    SHELDRAKE
                  (*into phone*)
The reason I called is – I won't be home for dinner tonight.
The branch manager from Kansas City is in town – I'm
taking him to the theatre – *Music Man*, what else? No, don't
wait up for me – 'bye, darling.
                  (*hangs up, turns to Bud*)
Tell me something, Baxter – have you seen *Music Man*?

                    BUD
Not yet. But I hear it's one swell show.

                    SHELDRAKE
How would you like to go tonight?

                    BUD
You mean – you and me? I thought you were taking the
branch manager from Kansas City –

                    SHELDRAKE
I made other plans. You can have both tickets.

                    BUD
Well, that's very kind of you – only I'm not feeling well – you
see, I have this cold – and I thought I'd go straight home.

SHELDRAKE

Baxter, you're not reading me. I told you I have plans.

BUD

So do I – I'm going to take four aspirins and get into bed – so
you better give the tickets to somebody else –

SHELDRAKE

I'm not just *giving* those tickets, Baxter – I want to *swap* them.

BUD

Swap them? For what?

Sheldrake picks up the Dobisch reports, puts on his glasses, turns a page.

SHELDRAKE

It also says here – that you are alert, astute, and quite
imaginative –

BUD

Oh?
                    (*the dawn is breaking*)
Oh!

*He reaches into his coat pocket, fishes out a handful of Kleenex, and
then finally the key to his apartment. He holds it up.*

BUD

This?

SHELDRAKE

That's good thinking, Baxter. Next month there's going to be
a shift in personnel around here – and as far as I'm
concerned, you're executive material.

BUD

I am?

SHELDRAKE

Now put down the key –
                    (*pushing a pad toward him*)
– and put down the address.

*Bud lays the key on the desk, unclips what he thinks is his fountain pen,
uncaps it, starts writing on the pad.*

It's on the second floor – my name is not on the door – it just says 2A –

Suddenly he realizes that he has been trying to write the address with the thermometer.

BUD

Oh – terribly sorry. It's that cold –

SHELDRAKE

Relax, Baxter.

BUD

Thank you sir.

He has replaced the thermometer with the fountain pen, and is scribbling the address.

You'll be careful with the record player, won't you? And about the liquor – I ordered some this morning – but I'm not sure when they'll deliver it –

He has finished writing the address, shoves the pad over to Sheldrake.

SHELDRAKE

Now remember, Baxter – this is going to be our little secret.

BUD

Yes, of course.

SHELDRAKE

You know how people talk.

BUD

Oh, you don't have to worry –

SHELDRAKE

Not that I have anything to hide.

BUD

Oh, no sir. Certainly not. Anyway, it's none of my business – four apples, five apples – what's the difference – percentage-wise?

SHELDRAKE
(*holding out the tickets*)
Here you are, Baxter. Have a nice time.

BUD
You too, sir.

Clutching the tickets, he backs out of the office.

DISSOLVE TO:

INT. LOBBY INSURANCE BUILDING – EVENING

*It is about 6:30, and the building has pretty well emptied out by now.
Bud, in raincoat and hat, is leaning against one of the marble pillars
beyond the elevators. His raincoat is unbuttoned, and Fran's carnation
is still in his lapel. He is looking off expectantly toward a door marked
EMPLOYEES' LOUNGE – WOMEN.*

*Some of the female employees are emerging, dressed for the street.
Among them are Sylvia and her colleague from the switchboard.*

SYLVIA
So I figure, a man in his position, he's going to take me to 21
and El Morocco – instead, he takes me to Hamburg Heaven
and some schnook's apartment –

*They pass Bud without paying any attention to him. Bud has heard the
crack, and looks after Sylvia, a little hurt. Then he glances back toward
the door of the lounge, as it opens and Fran Kubelik comes out. She is
wearing a wool coat over a street dress, no hat.*

FRAN
(*passing Bud*)
Good night.

BUD
(*casually*)
Good night.

She is about three paces beyond him when he suddenly realizes who it is.
Oh – Miss Kubelik.
(*he rushes after her, taking off his hat*)
I've been waiting for you.

47

FRAN

You have?

BUD

I almost didn't recognize you – this is the first time I've ever seen you in civilian clothes.

FRAN

How'd you make out on the twenty-seventh floor?

BUD

Great. Look – have you seen *The Music Man?*

FRAN

No.

BUD

Would you like to?

FRAN

Sure.

                              BUD
I thought maybe we could have a bite to eat first – and then –

                             FRAN
You mean tonight?

                              BUD
Yeah.

                             FRAN
I'm sorry, but I can't tonight. I'm meeting somebody.

                              BUD
Oh.
                           (*a beat*)
You mean – like a girl-friend?

                             FRAN
No. Like a man.

She proceeds across the lobby toward the street entrance, Bud following her.

                              BUD
I wasn't trying to be personal – it's just that the fellows in the office were wondering about you – whether you ever –

                             FRAN
Just tell 'em – now and then.

                              BUD
This date – is it just a date – or is it something serious?

                             FRAN
It *used* to be serious – at least *I* was – but he wasn't – so the whole thing is more or less kaput.

                              BUD
Well, in that case, couldn't you – ?

                             FRAN
I'm afraid not. I promised to have a drink with him – he's been calling me all week –

                               49

BUD

Oh, I understand.

He follows her out through the revolving doors.

EXT. INSURANCE BUILDING – EVENING

Fran and Bud come out.

BUD
(putting his hat on)
Well, it was just an idea – I hate to see a ticket go to waste –

FRAN
(stops)
What time does the show go on?

BUD

Eight-thirty.

FRAN
(looks at her watch)
Well – I could meet you at the theatre – if that's all right.

BUD
All right? That's wonderful! It's the Majestic – 44th Street.

FRAN
Meet you in the lobby. Okay?

Bud nods happily, falls in beside her as she starts down the street.

BUD
You know, I felt so lousy this morning – a hundred and one
fever – then my promotion came up – now you and I –
eleventh row center – and you said I should have stayed in
bed.

FRAN
How *is* your cold?

BUD
(high as a kite)
What cold? And after the show, we could go out on the town –

                    (*does a little cha-cha step*)
I've been taking from Arthur Murray.

FRAN

So I see.

BUD

They got a great little band at El Chico, in the Village – it's practically around the corner from where you live.

FRAN

Sounds good.
                    (*a sudden thought*)
How do you know where I live?

BUD

Oh, I even know who you live *with* – your sister and brother-in-law – I know when you were born – and where – I know all sorts of things about you.

FRAN

How come?

BUD

A couple of months ago I looked up your card in the group insurance file.

FRAN

Oh.

BUD

I know your height, your weight and your Social Security number – you had mumps, you had measles, and you had your appendix out.

They have now reached the corner, and Fran stops.

FRAN

Well, don't tell the fellows in the office about the appendix. They may get the wrong idea how you found out.
                    (*turning the corner*)
'Bye.

(*calling after her*)

Eight-thirty!

He watches her walk away, an idiot grin on his face. Despite what he told Fran, his nose is stuffed up, so he takes out the anti-histamine and sprays his nostrils. Then, carried away, he squirts some of the stuff on the carnation in his buttonhole, moves off in the opposite direction.

EXT. DOWNTOWN STREET – EVENING

Fran comes hurrying along the street. She is late. Her objective is a small Chinese restaurant, with a neon sign reading THE RICKSHAW – COCKTAILS – CANTONESE FOOD. *She starts down a flight of steps leading to the entrance.*

INT. CHINESE RESTAURANT – EVENING

The bar is a long, narrow, dimly-lit room with booths along one side. Beyond a bamboo curtain is the main dining room, which does not concern us. The place is decorated in Early Beachcomber style – rattan, fish-nets, conch shells, etc.

The help is Chinese. At this early hour, there are only half a dozen customers in the place – all at the bar except for one man, sitting in the last booth with his back toward camera. At a piano, a Chinese member of Local 808 is improvising mood music.

Fran comes through the door, and without looking around, heads straight for the last booth. The bartender nods to her – they know her there. As she passes the piano player, he gives her a big smile, segues into 'Jealous Lover'

Fran comes up to the man sitting in the last booth.

FRAN
(*a wistful smile*)

Good evening, Mr Sheldrake.

Sheldrake, for that's who it is, looks around nervously to make sure no one has heard her.

SHELDRAKE

Please, Fran – not so loud.

He gets up.

FRAN

Still afraid somebody may see us together?

SHELDRAKE
(*reaching for her coat*)

Let me take that.

FRAN

No, Jeff. I can't stay very long.
(*sits opposite him, with her coat on*)
Can I have a frozen daiquiri?

SHELDRAKE

It's on the way.
(*sits down*)
I see you went ahead and cut your hair.

FRAN

That's right.

SHELDRAKE

You know I liked it better long.

FRAN

Yes, I know. You want a lock to carry in your wallet?

A waiter comes up with a tray: two daiquiris, fried shrimp, eggrolls, and a bowl of sauce.

WAITER
(*showing all his teeth*)

Evening, lady. Nice see you again.

FRAN

Thank you.

The waiter has set everything on the table, leaves.

SHELDRAKE

How long has it been – a month?

FRAN

Six weeks. But who's counting?

SHELDRAKE

I missed you, Fran.

FRAN

Like old times. Same booth, same song –

SHELDRAKE

It's been hell.

FRAN
(*dipping shrimp*)
– same sauce – sweet and sour.

SHELDRAKE

You don't know what it's like – standing next to you in that
elevator, day after day – Good morning, Miss Kubelik –
Good night, Mr Sheldrake – I'm still crazy about you, Fran.

FRAN
(*avoiding his eyes*)
Let's not start on that again, Jeff – *please*. I'm just beginning
to get over it.

SHELDRAKE

I don't believe you.

FRAN

Look, Jeff – we had two wonderful months this summer – and
that was it. Happens all the time – the wife and kids go away
to the country, and the boss has a fling with the secretary – or
the manicurist – or the elevator girl. Comes September, the
picnic is over – goodbye. The kids go back to school, the boss
goes back to the wife, and the girl –
(*she is barely able to control herself*)
They don't make these shrimp like they used to.

SHELDRAKE

I never said goodbye, Fran.

FRAN
(*not listening*)

For a while there, you try kidding yourself that you're going
with an unmarried man. Then one day he keeps looking at
his watch, and asks you if there's any lipstick showing, then
rushes off to catch the seven-fourteen to White Plains. So you
fix yourself a cup of instant coffee – and you sit there by
yourself – and you think – and it all begins to look so ugly –

*There are tears in her eyes. She breaks off, downs what's left of the
daiquiri.*

SHELDRAKE

How do you think *I* felt – riding home on that seven-fourteen
train?

FRAN

Why do you keep calling me, Jeff? What do you want from
me?

SHELDRAKE
(*taking her hand*)

I want you back, Fran.

FRAN
(*withdrawing her hand*)

Sorry, Mr Sheldrake – I'm full up. You'll have to take the
next elevator.

SHELDRAKE

You're not giving me a chance, Fran. I asked you to meet me
because – I have something to tell you.

FRAN

Go ahead – tell me.

SHELDRAKE
(*a glance around*)

Not here, Fran. Can't we go some place else?

FRAN

No. I have a date at eight-thirty.

Important?

FRAN

Not very – but I'm going to be there anyway.

She takes out an inexpensive square compact with a fleur-de-lis pattern on it, opens it, starts to fix her face. The waiter comes up with a couple of menus.

WAITER

You ready order dinner now?

FRAN

No. No dinner.

SHELDRAKE

Bring us two more drinks.

CUT TO:

EXT. MAJESTIC THEATRE – EVENING

It is 8:25, and there is the usual hectic to-do – taxis pulling up, people milling around the sidewalk and crowding into the lobby. In the middle of this mêlée, buffeted by the throng, stands Bud, in raincoat and hat, looking anxiously for Fran.

CUT TO:

INT. CHINESE RESTAURANT – EVENING

Fran and Sheldrake, in the booth, are working on the second round of drinks.

SHELDRAKE

Fran – remember that last weekend we had?

FRAN
(*wryly*)

Do I. That leaky little boat you rented – and me in a black negligée and a life preserver –

SHELDRAKE

Remember what we talked about?

56

                    FRAN
We talked about a lot of things.

                  SHELDRAKE
I mean – about my getting a divorce.

                    FRAN
We didn't talk about it – *you* did.

                  SHELDRAKE
You didn't really believe me, did you?

                    FRAN
                 (*shrugging*)
They got it on a long-playing record now – 'Music to String
Her Along By'. My wife doesn't understand me – We haven't
gotten along for years – You're the best thing that ever
happened to me –

                  SHELDRAKE
That's enough, Fran.

                    FRAN
               (*going right on*)
Just trust me, baby – we'll work it out somehow –

                  SHELDRAKE
You're not being funny.

                    FRAN
I wasn't trying.

                  SHELDRAKE
If you'll just listen to me for a minute –

                    FRAN
Okay. I'm sorry.

                  SHELDRAKE
I saw my lawyer this morning – I wanted his advice – about
the best way to handle it –

                    FRAN
Handle what?

SHELDRAKE
What do you think?

FRAN
(*looking at him for a long moment – then*)
Let's get something straight, Jeff – I never asked you to leave
your wife.

SHELDRAKE
Of course not. You had nothing to do with it.

FRAN
(*her eyes misting up again*)
Are you sure that's what you want?

SHELDRAKE
I'm sure. If you'll just tell me that you still love me –

FRAN
(*softly*)
You know I do.

SHELDRAKE
Fran –

*He takes her hand, kisses it. The bar has been filling up, and now two
couples are seating themselves in a nearby booth. One of the women is
Miss Olsen.*

FRAN
(*pulling her hand away gently*)
Jeff – darling –

*She indicates the other customers. Sheldrake glances over his
shoulder.*

SHELDRAKE
It *is* crowding up. Let's get out of here.

*They rise. Sheldrake leaves some money on the table, leads Fran toward
the entrance. As they pass Miss Olsen's booth, she turns around slowly,
and putting on her glasses, looks after them.*

Sheldrake slips a bill to the piano player, who gives them a big smile, slides into 'Jealous Lover' again. Retrieving his hat and coat from the checkroom girl, Sheldrake steers Fran through the door.

Miss Olsen watches them with a cold smile.

EXT. CHINESE RESTAURANT – EVENING

Fran and Sheldrake come up the steps.

> SHELDRAKE
> (*to a passing cab*)

Taxi!

It passes without stopping.

> FRAN

I have that date – remember?

> SHELDRAKE

I love you – remember?

Another taxi approaches. Sheldrake gives a shrill whistle, and it pulls up. He opens the door.

> FRAN

Where are we going, Jeff? Not back to that leaky boat –

> SHELDRAKE

I promise.

He helps her into the cab, takes out of his coat pocket the page from the pad on which Bud wrote the address of the apartment.

> SHELDRAKE
> (*to cab driver*)

51 West Sixty-Seventh.

He gets in beside Fran, shuts the door. As the cab pulls away, through the rear window the two can be seen kissing.

CUT TO:

EXT. MAJESTIC THEATRE – EVENING

It's 9 o'clock, the lobby is deserted, and standing on the sidewalk all by

himself, is Bud. He takes a Kleenex out of his pocket, blows his nose,
stuffs the used Kleenex in another pocket. He looks up and down the
street, consults his watch, decides to wait just a little longer.

FADE OUT:

FADE IN:

BAXTER'S DESK CALENDAR

The leaves are flipping over. Mr Sheldrake seems to be using the
Apartment regularly – for the name 'Sheldrake', in Bud's
handwriting, appears on the pages dated Monday, November 9,
Thursday, November 12, Thursday, November 19, Monday,
November 23, and Monday, November 30. Mr Sheldrake also seems
to be Baxter's only customer by now, since the other leaves of the
calendar are blank.

DISSOLVE TO:

INT. NINETEENTH FLOOR – INSURANCE BUILDING – DAY

It is a gloomy December morning, and hundreds of desk-bound
employees are bent over their paper work.

Bud Baxter, in raincoat and hat, is clearing out his desk. He has piled
everything on his blotter pad – reference books, papers, a fountain-pen
set, pencils, paper clips and the calendar. Watching him from the next
desk is a dumbfounded Moffett. Bud picks up the blotter pad with his
stuff on it, and as he moves past Moffett's desk, Moffett takes out a
dollar bill, drops it grudgingly on the loaded pad. Bud flashes him a
little grin, continues between the desks toward the row of glass-enclosed
offices housing the supervisory personnel.

He comes up to an unoccupied cubicle. A sign painter is brushing in
some new lettering on the glass door – it reads C. C. BAXTER, SECOND
ADMINISTRATIVE ASSISTANT. Bud studies the sign with a good deal
of satisfaction.

BUD

(to painter)

Would you mind – ?

(the painter turns around)

C. C. Baxter – that's me.

With an 'Oh', the painter opens the door for him.

INT. BAXTER'S OFFICE – DAY

Bud enters his new office, deposits his stuff on the bare desk, looks around possessively. The small cubicle boasts one window, carpeting on the floor, a filing cabinet, a couple of synthetic-leather chairs, and a clothes-tree – to Bud, it is the Taj Mahal. He crosses to the clothes-tree, removes his hat and coat, hangs them up. From Off comes –

KIRKEBY'S VOICE

Hi, Buddy-boy.

DOBISCH'S VOICE

Congratulations, and all that jazz.

Bud turns. Kirkeby, Dobisch, Eichelberger and Vanderhof have come into the office.

> BUD
>
> Hi, fellas.

> EICHELBERGER
>
> Well, you made it, kid – just like we promised.

> VANDERHOF
>
> Quite an office – name on the door – rug on the floor – the whole schmear.

> BUD
>
> Yeah.

> DOBISCH
>
> Teamwork – that's what counts in an organization like this. All for one and one for all – know what I mean?

> BUD
>
> I have a vague idea.

Kirkeby signals to Vanderhof, who shuts the door. The four charter members of the club start closing in on Bud.

> KIRKEBY
>
> Baxter, we're a little disappointed in you – gratitude-wise.

> BUD
>
> Oh, I'm very grateful.

> EICHELBERGER
>
> Then why are you locking us out, all of a sudden?

> BUD
>
> It's been sort of rough these last few weeks – what with my cold and like that –

He has picked up the desk calendar, shoves it discreetly into one of the drawers.

> DOBISCH
>
> We went to bat for you – and now you won't play ball with us.

BUD

Well, after all, it's my apartment – it's private property – it's not a public playground.

VANDERHOF

All right, so you got yourself a girl – that's okay with us – but not every night of the week.

KIRKEBY

How selfish can you get?
(*to the others*)
Last week I had to borrow my nephew's car and take Sylvia to a drive-in in Jersey. I'm too old for that sort of thing – I mean, in a Volkswagen.

BUD

I sympathize with your problem – and believe me, I'm very sorry –

DOBISCH

You'll be a lot sorrier before we're through with you.

BUD

You threatening me?

DOBISCH

Listen, Baxter, we made you and we can break you.

He deliberately flips a cigar ash on Bud's desk. At the same time, the door opens, and Sheldrake comes striding in briskly.

BUD

Good morning, Mr Sheldrake.

The others swivel around.

SHELDRAKE

Morning, gentlemen.
(*to Bud*)
Everything satisfactory? You like your office?

BUD

Oh, yes, sir. Very much. And I want to thank you –

SHELDRAKE

Don't thank me – thank your friends here – they're the ones who recommended you.

The four friends manage to work up some sickly smiles.

DOBISCH

We just dropped in to wish him the best.
        (*quickly brushes cigar ash off desk*)

KIRKEBY

        (*as they move toward the door*)
So long, Baxter. We know you won't let us down.

BUD

So long fellas. Drop in any time. The door is always open – to my office.

They leave. Sheldrake and Bud are alone.

SHELDRAKE

I like the way you handled that. Well how does it feel to be an executive?

BUD

Fine. And I want you to know I'll work very hard to justify your confidence in me –

SHELDRAKE

Sure you will.
(*a beat*)
Say, Baxter, about the apartment – now that you got a raise, don't you think we can afford a *second* key?

BUD

Well – I guess so.

SHELDRAKE

You know my secretary – Miss Olsen –

BUD

Oh, yes. Very attractive. Is she – the lucky one?

SHELDRAKE

No, you don't understand. She's a busybody – always poking her nose into things – and with that key passing back and forth – why take chances?

BUD

Yes, sir. You can't be too careful.

He glances toward the glass partitions to make sure that nobody is watching.

I have something here – I think it belongs to you.

Out of his pocket he has slipped the compact with the fleur-de-lis pattern we saw Fran use at the Rickshaw. He holds it out to Sheldrake.

SHELDRAKE

To me?

BUD

I mean – the young lady – whoever she may be – it was on the couch when I got home last night.

65

SHELDRAKE

Oh, yes. Thanks.

BUD

The mirror is broken.
> (*opens compact, revealing crack in mirror*)

It was broken when I found it.

SHELDRAKE

So it was.
> (*takes the compact*)

She threw it at me.

BUD

Sir?

SHELDRAKE

You know how it is – sooner or later they all give you a bad time.

BUD
> (*man-of-the-world*)

I know how it is.

SHELDRAKE

You see a girl a couple of times a week – just for laughs – and right away she thinks you're going to divorce your wife. I ask you – is that fair?

BUD

No, sir. That's very unfair – especially to your wife.

SHELDRAKE

Yeah.
> (*shifting gears*)

You know, Baxter, I envy you. Bachelor – all the dames you want – no headaches, no complications –

BUD

Yes, sir. That's the life, all right.

SHELDRAKE

Put me down for Thursday again.

BUD

Roger. And I'll get that other key.

Sheldrake exits. Bud takes the calendar out of the desk drawer, makes an entry.

BAXTER'S DESK CALENDAR

Again the leaves are flipping over, and again we see Sheldrake's name in Bud's handwriting – booked for the following dates: Monday, December 14, Thursday, December 17, Monday, December 21, Thursday, December 24.

DISSOLVE TO:

INT. SWITCHBOARD ROOM – DAY

Perched on top of the switchboard is a small decorated Christmas tree, and the operators are dispensing holiday greetings to all callers.

OPERATORS

Consolidated Life – Merry Christmas – I'll connect you –
Consolidated Life – Merry Christmas – I'm ringing –

In the foreground, Sylvia is engaged in a private conversation of her own.

SYLVIA
(into mouthpiece)

Yeah? – *Yeah?* – Where? – You bet –

She tears off her headset, and turns to the other girls.

Somebody watch my line – there's a swinging party up on the nineteenth floor –

She scoots out the door. The other girls immediately abandon their posts, and dash after her.

INT. NINETEENTH FLOOR – DAY

It's a swinging party, all right. Nobody is working. Several desks have been cleared and pushed together, and on top of this improvised stage four female employees and Mr Dobisch, with his pants-legs rolled up,

*are doing a Rockette kick routine to the tune of 'Jingle Bells'. Employees
are ringed around the performers, some drinking out of paper cups,
others singing and clapping in rhythm.*

*One of the cubicles has been transformed into a bar, and it is jammed
with people. Mr Kirkeby and Mr Vanderhof are pouring – each has a
couple of bottles of liquor in his hands, and is emptying them into the
open top of a water-cooler. But the stuff is flowing out as fast as it flows
in – everybody is in line with a paper cup waiting for a refill.*

*Bud comes shouldering his way out of the crowded cubicle, holding aloft
two paper cups filled with booze. Since his promotion he has bought
himself a new suit, dark flannel, and with it he wears a white shirt with
a pinned round collar, and a foulard tie. He also has quite a glow on.
Detouring past necking couples, he heads in the direction of the
elevators.*

*The doors of Fran's elevator are just opening, and the switch-board
operators, led by Sylvia, come streaming out.*

SYLVIA
(*to a colleague*)
– so I said to him: Never again! – either get yourself a bigger
car or a smaller girl –

*As they head for the party, they pass Bud, who is approaching the
elevator with the two drinks. Fran is just closing the elevator doors.*

BUD
Miss Kubelik.

*The doors slide open again, and Fran looks out. Instead of the
customary carnation in the lapel of her uniform, she wears a sprig of
holly.*
(*holding out one of the drinks*)
Merry Christmas.

FRAN
Thank you.
(*takes drink*)
I thought you were avoiding me.

68

What gave you that idea?

FRAN

In the last six weeks you've only been in my elevator once –
and then you didn't take your hat off.

BUD

Well, as a matter of fact, I *was* rather hurt when you stood me
up that night –

FRAN

I don't blame you. It was unforgivable.

BUD

I forgive you.

FRAN

You shouldn't.

BUD

You couldn't help yourself. I mean, when you're having a
drink with *one* man, you can't just suddenly walk out on him
because you have *another* date with *another* man. You did the
only decent thing.

FRAN

Don't be too sure. Just because I wear a uniform – that
doesn't make me a Girl Scout.

BUD

Miss Kubelik, one doesn't get to be a second administrative
assistant around here unless he's a pretty good judge of
character – and as far as I'm concerned, you're tops, I mean,
decency-wise – and otherwise-wise.
                    (*toasting*)
Cheers.

FRAN

Cheers.

They down their drinks. Bud takes the empty cup from her.

BUD

One more?

FRAN
(*indicating elevator*)
I shouldn't drink when I'm driving.

BUD

You're so right.

He reaches into the elevator, takes a cardboard sign off a hook, hangs it on the elevator door. It reads USE OTHER ELEVATOR.

BUD

By the power vested in me, I herewith declare this elevator out of order.
(*leading her toward the party*)
Shall we join the natives?

FRAN

Why not?
(*as they pass a kissing couple*)
They seem friendly enough.

BUD

Don't you believe it. Later on there will be human sacrifices – white-collar workers tossed into the computing machines, and punched full of those little square holes.

FRAN

How many of those drinks did you have?

BUD
(*holding up four fingers*)
Three.

FRAN

I thought so.

They have now reached the entrance to the bar, which is overflowing with thirsty natives.

BUD

You wait here. I think I hear the sound of running water.

He leaves her outside the cubicle, and elbows his way through the crowd toward the booze-filled water cooler. Out of another cubicle comes Miss Olsen, cup in hand. She too has had quite a few. Seeing Fran, she walks up to her, with an acid smile on her face.

MISS OLSEN

Hi. How's the branch manager from Kansas City?

FRAN

I beg your pardon?

MISS OLSEN

I'm Miss Olsen – Mr Sheldrake's secretary.

FRAN

Yes, I know.

MISS OLSEN

So you don't have to play innocent with me. He used to tell his wife that I was the branch manager from Seattle – four years ago when *we* were having a little ring-a-ding-ding.

FRAN

I don't know what you're talking about.

MISS OLSEN

And before me there was Miss Rossi in Auditing – and after me there was Miss Koch in Disability – and just before you there was Miss What's-Her-Name, on the twenty-fifth floor –

FRAN
(*wanting to get away*)

Will you excuse me?

MISS OLSEN
(*holding her by the arm*)

What for? You haven't done anything – it's him – what a salesman – always the last booth in the Chinese restaurant – and the same pitch about divorcing his wife – and in the end you wind up with egg foo yong on your face.

Bud comes burrowing out of the crowded cubicle, balancing the two filled paper cups, spots Fran.

                                  BUD

Miss Kubelik.

Fran turns away from Miss Olsen.

                                  FRAN

Well – thank you.

                               MISS OLSEN

Always happy to do something for our girls in uniform.

She moves off as Bud joins Fran, who is looking a little pale.

                                  BUD

You all right? What's the matter?

                                  FRAN

Nothing.
                            (*takes the drink*)
There are just too many people here.

                                  BUD

Why don't we step into my office? There's something I want
your advice about, anyway.
                       (*leads her toward his cubicle*)
I have my own office now, naturally. And you may be
interested to know I'm the second-youngest executive in
the company – the only one younger is a grandson of the
chairman of the board.

INT. BAXTER'S OFFICE – DAY

*Bud ushers Fran in, and is confronted by a strange couple necking in the
corner. He gestures them out, crosses to his desk.*

                                  BUD

Miss Kubelik, I would like your honest opinion. I've had this
in my desk for a week – cost me fifteen dollars – but I just
couldn't get up enough nerve to wear it –

*From under the desk he has produced a hatbox, and out of the hatbox a
black bowler, which he now puts on his head.*

It's what they call the junior executive model. What do you
think?

                                    72

Fran looks at him blankly, absorbed in her own thoughts.

Guess I made a boo-boo, huh?

FRAN
(*paying attention again*)

No – I like it.

BUD

Really? You mean you wouldn't be ashamed to be seen with somebody in a hat like this?

FRAN

Of course not.

BUD

Maybe if I wore it a little more to the side –
(*adjusting hat*)
– is that better?

FRAN

Much better.

BUD

Well, as long as you wouldn't be ashamed to be seen with me – how about the three of us going out this evening – you and me and the bowler – stroll down Fifth Avenue – sort of break it in –

FRAN

This is a bad day for me.

BUD

I understand. Christmas – family and all that –

FRAN

I'd better get back to my elevator. I don't want to be fired.

BUD

Oh, you don't have to worry about that. I have quite a bit of influence in Personnel. You know Mr Sheldrake?

FRAN
(*guardedly*)

Why?

He and I are like this.
>(*crosses his fingers*)
Sent me a Christmas card. See?

He has picked up a Christmas card from his desk, shows it to Fran. It is a photograph of the Sheldrake clan grouped around an elaborate Christmas tree – Mr and Mrs Sheldrake, the two boys in military school uniforms, and a big French poodle. Underneath it says:

>SEASON'S GREETINGS
>from the SHELDRAKES
>Emily, Jeff, Tommy, Jeff Jr,
>and Figaro.

FRAN
>(*studying the card ruefully*)
Makes a cute picture.

BUD
I thought maybe I could put in a word for you with Mr Sheldrake – get you a little promotion – how would you like to be an elevator starter?

FRAN
I'm afraid there are too many other girls around here with seniority over me.

BUD
No problem. Why don't we discuss it sometime over the holidays – I could call you and pick you up – and we'll have the big unveiling –
>(*touching the brim of his bowler*)
– you sure this is the right way to wear it?

FRAN
I think so.

BUD
You don't think it's tilted a little *too* much –

Fran takes her compact out of her uniform pocket, opens it, hands it to Bud.

74

FRAN

Here.

BUD

(*examining himself in the mirror*)

After all, this is a conservative firm – I don't want people to think I'm an entertainer –

His voice trails off. There is something familiar about the cracked mirror of the compact – and the fleur-de-lis pattern on the case confirms his suspicion. Fran notices the peculiar expression on his face.

FRAN

What is it?

BUD

(*with difficulty*)

The mirror – it's broken.

FRAN

I know. I like it this way – makes me look the way I feel.

The phone has started to ring. Bud doesn't hear it. He closes the compact, hands it to Fran.

FRAN

Your phone.

BUD

Oh.

(*picks up phone from desk*)

Yes?

(*throws a quick look at Fran*)

Just a minute.

(*covers mouthpiece; to Fran*)

If you don't mind – this is sort of personal.

FRAN

All right. Have a nice Christmas.

She exits, closing the door. Bud takes his hand off the mouthpiece.

BUD
(every word hurts)

Yes, Mr Sheldrake – no, I didn't forget – the tree is up and the Tom and Jerry mix is in the refrigerator – yes, sir – same to you.

He hangs up, stands there for a moment, the bowler still on his head, the noise from the party washing over him. He slowly crosses to the clothes-tree, picks up his coat – a new, black chesterfield. With the coat over his arm, he starts out of the office.

INT. NINETEENTH FLOOR – DAY

The party has picked up tempo. On top of the desks, Sylvia is doing a mock strip tease – without taking any clothes off. There is hollering, drinking and clapping all around her.

Bud moves past the floor show, paying no attention. Kirkeby spots him, detaches himself from the cheering section around Sylvia.

KIRKEBY

Where you going, Buddy-boy? The party's just starting.
(catching up with him)

Listen, kid – give me a break, will you – how about tomorrow afternoon? I can't take her to that drive-in again – the car doesn't even have a heater – four o'clock – okay?

Bud ignores him, continues walking through the ranks of empty desks.

DISSOLVE TO:

INT. CHEAP BAR – COLUMBUS AVENUE IN THE SIXTIES – EVENING

It is six o'clock, and the joint is crowded with customers having one for the road before joining their families for Christmas Eve. There are men with gaily wrapped packages, small trussed-up Christmas trees, a plucked turkey in a plastic bag. Written across the mirror behind the bar, in glittering white letters, is HAPPY HOLIDAYS. Everybody is in high spirits, laughing it up and toasting each other.

Everybody except Bud Baxter. He is standing at the bar in his chesterfield and bowler, slightly isolated, brooding over an almost empty martini glass. The bartender comes up, sets down a fresh martini with

76

an olive on a toothpick, takes his payment from a pile of bills and coins lying in front of Bud. Bud fishes out the olive, adds it to a half a dozen other impaled olives neatly arranged in fan shape on the counter. He is obviously trying to complete the circle.

A short, rotund man dressed as Santa Claus hurries in from the street, and comes up to the bar beside Bud.

SANTA CLAUS
(to bartender)

Hey, Charlie – give me a shot of bourbon – and step on it – my sleigh is double parked.

He laughs uproariously at his own joke, nudges Bud with his elbow. Bud stares at him coldly, turns back to his martini. The laughter dies in Santa Claus' throat. He gets his shot of bourbon, moves down the bar to find more convivial company.

Standing near the end of the curved bar is a girl in her middle twenties wearing a ratty fur coat. Her name is Margie MacDougall, she is drinking a Rum Collins through a straw, and she too is alone. From a distance, she is studying Bud with interest. On the bar in front of her is a container of straws in paper wrappers. She takes one of them out, tears off the end of the paper, blows through the straw – sending the wrapper floating toward Bud. The paper wrapper passes right in front of Bud's nose. He doesn't notice it.

Margie, undaunted, lets go with another missile.

This time the wrapper lands on the brim of Bud's bowler. No reaction. Another wrapper comes floating in, hits Bud's cheek. He never takes his eye off his martini.

Margie leaves her place, and carrying her handbag and her empty glass, comes up alongside Bud. Without a word, she reaches up and removes the wrapper from Bud's bowler.

MARGIE

You buy me a drink, I'll buy you some music.
(sets the glass down)
Rum Collins.

Not waiting for an answer, she heads for the juke box. Bud looks after her noncommittally, then turns to the bartender.

BUD

Rum Collins.
(indicating martini glass)
And another one of these little mothers.

At the juke box, Margie has dropped a coin in and made her selection. The music starts – 'Adeste Fideles'. She rejoins Bud at the bar just as the bartender is putting down their drinks in front of them. Bud removes the new olive, adds it to the pattern on the counter in front of him. They both drink, staring straight ahead. For quite a while, there is complete silence between them.

MARGIE
(out of nowhere)

You like Castro?
(a blank look from Bud)
I mean – how do you feel about Castro?

78

BUD

What is Castro?

MARGIE

You know, that big-shot down in Cuba – with the crazy
beard.

BUD

What about him?

MARGIE

Because as far as I'm concerned, he's a no-good fink. Two
weeks ago I wrote him a letter – never even answered me.

BUD

That so.

MARGIE

All I wanted him to do was let Mickey out for Christmas.

BUD

Who is Mickey?

MARGIE

My husband. He's in Havana – in jail.

BUD

Oh. Mixed up in that revolution?

MARGIE

Mickey? He wouldn't do nothing like that. He's a jockey.
They caught him doping a horse.

BUD

Well, you can't win 'em all.

*They sit there silently for a moment, contemplating the injustices of the
world.*

MARGIE
(*to herself*)
'Twas the night before Christmas
And all through the house
Not a creature was stirring –
Nothing –

No action—
Dullsville!

> (*drinks; to Bud*)

You married?

BUD

No.

MARGIE

Family?

BUD

No.

MARGIE

A night like this, it sort of spooks you to walk into an empty apartment.

BUD

I said I had no family – I didn't say I had an empty apartment.

They both drink.

CUT TO:

INT. BUD'S APARTMENT – EVENING

The living room is dark, except for a shaft of light from the kitchen, and the glow of the colored bulbs on a small Christmas tree in front of the phony fireplace.

Hunched up in one corner of the couch is Fran, still in her coat and gloves, crying softly. Pacing up and down is Sheldrake. His coat and hat are on a chair, as are several Christmas packages. On the coffee table are an unopened bottle of Scotch, a couple of untouched glasses, and a bowl of melting ice.

SHELDRAKE
> (*stops and faces Fran*)

Come on, Fran – don't be like that. You just going to sit there and keep bawling?

> (*no answer*)

You won't talk to me, you won't tell me what's wrong –

(*a new approach*)
Look, I know you think I'm stalling you. But when you've
been married to a woman for twelve years, you don't just sit
down at the breakfast table and say 'Pass the sugar – and I
want a divorce.' It's not that easy.

He resumes pacing: Fran continues crying.

Anyway, this is the wrong time. The kids are home from
school – my in-laws are visiting for the holidays – I can't bring
it up *now*.
(*stops in front of her*)
This isn't like you, Fran – you were always such a good sport
– such fun to be with –

FRAN
(*through tears*)
Yeah – that's me. The Happy Idiot – a million laughs.

SHELDRAKE
Well, that's more like it. At least you're speaking to me.

Funny thing happened to me at the office party today – I ran
into your secretary – Miss Olsen. You know – ring-a-ding-
ding? I laughed so much I like to died.

SHELDRAKE

Is that what's been bothering you – Miss Olsen? That's
ancient history.

FRAN

I was never very good at history. Let me see – there was Miss
Olsen, and then there was Miss Rossi – no, she came before –
it was Miss Koch who came after Miss Olsen –

SHELDRAKE

Now, Fran –

FRAN

And just think – right now there's some lucky girl in the
building who's going to come after me –

SHELDRAKE

Okay, okay, Fran. I deserve that. But just ask yourself – why
does a man run around with a lot of girls? Because he's
unhappy at home – because he's lonely, that's why – all that
was before you, Fran – I've stopped running.

Fran has taken a handkerchief out of her bag and is dabbing her eyes.

FRAN

How could I be so stupid? You'd think I would have learned
by now – when you're in love with a married man, you
shouldn't wear mascara.

SHELDRAKE

It's Christmas Eve, Fran – let's not fight.

FRAN

Merry Christmas.

She hands him a flat, wrapped package.

SHELDRAKE

What is it?

He strips away the wrapping to reveal a long-playing record. The cover reads: 'Rickshaw Boy – Jimmy Lee Kiang with Orchestra'.

Oh. Our friend from the Chinese restaurant. Thanks, Fran. We better keep it here.

FRAN

Yeah, we better.

SHELDRAKE

I have a present for *you*. I didn't quite know what to get you – anyway it's a little awkward for me, shopping –
>(*he has taken out a money clip, detaches a bill*)

– so here's a hundred dollars – go out and buy yourself something.

He holds the money out, but she doesn't move. Sheldrake slips the bill into her open bag.

They have some nice alligator bags at Bergdorf's –

Fran gets up slowly and starts peeling off her gloves. Sheldrake looks at her, then glances nervously at his wrist watch.

Fran, it's a quarter to seven – and I mustn't miss the train – if we hadn't wasted all that time – I have to get home and trim the tree –

Fran has started to remove her coat.

FRAN

Okay.
>(*shrugs the coat back on*)

I just thought as long as it was paid for –

SHELDRAKE
>(*an angry step toward her*)

Don't ever talk like that, Fran! Don't make yourself out to be cheap.

FRAN

A hundred dollars? I wouldn't call that cheap. And you must be paying somebody something for the use of the apartment –

83

SHELDRAKE
(*grabbing her arms*)
Stop that, Fran.

FRAN
(*quietly*)
You'll miss your train, Jeff.

Sheldrake hurriedly puts on his hat and coat, gathers up his packages.

SHELDRAKE
Coming?

FRAN
You run along – I want to fix my face.

SHELDRAKE
(*heading for the door*)
Don't forget to kill the lights. See you Monday.

FRAN
Sure. Monday and Thursday - and Monday again - and
Thursday again –

SHELDRAKE
(*that stops him in the half-open door*)
It won't always be like this.
(*coming back*)
I love you, Fran.

Holding the packages to one side, he tries to kiss her on the mouth.

FRAN
(*turning her head*)
Careful – lipstick.

He kisses her on the cheek, hurries out of the apartment, closing the door. Fran stands there for a while, blinking back tears, then takes the long-playing record out of its envelope, crosses to the phonograph. She puts the record on, starts the machine – the music is 'Jealous Lover'. As it plays, Fran wanders aimlessly around the darkened room, her body wracked with sobs. Finally she regains control of herself, and picking up her handbag, starts through the bedroom toward the bathroom.

In the bathroom, Fran switches on the light, puts her bag on the sink, turns on the faucet. Scooping up some water, she washes the smeared mascara away, then turns the faucet off, picks up a towel. As she is drying her face, she notices in the pull-away shaving mirror the magnified reflection of a vial of pills on the medicine shelf. Fran reaches out for the vial, turns it slowly around in her hand. The label reads:
SECONAL — ONE AT BEDTIME AS NEEDED FOR SLEEP.

Fran studies the label for a second, then returns the vial to the shelf. She opens her handbag, takes out a lipstick. As she does so, she sees the hundred dollar bill Sheldrake left in the bag. Her eyes wander back to the vial on the medicine shelf. Then very deliberately she picks up Bud's mouthwash glass, removes the two toothbrushes from it, turns on the faucet, starts filling the glass with water.

DISSOLVE TO:

INT. CHEAP BAR — COLUMBUS AVENUE — NIGHT

The joint is deserted now except for the Santa Claus, who is leaning against the bar, quite loaded, and Bud and Margie MacDougall, who are dancing to a slow blues coming from the juke box. Bud is still in his overcoat and bowler, and Margie is wearing her fur coat. The bartender is sweeping up the place.

> BARTENDER
> (*to Santa Claus*)
> Drink up, Pop. It's closing time.

> SANTA CLAUS
> But it's early, Charlie.

> BARTENDER
> Don't you know what night this is?

> SANTA CLAUS
> I know, Charlie. I know. I work for the outfit.

He polishes off his drink, walks out unsteadily. The bartender approaches the dancers.

> BARTENDER
> Hey, knock it off, will you? Go home.

Bud and Margie ignore him, continue dancing – or rather swaying limply cheek-to-cheek. The bartender crosses to the juke box, pulls the plug out. The music stops, but not Bud and Margie – they continue dancing.

O-U-T – out!

He goes to the front of the bar, starts to extinguish the lights. Margie picks up her handbag from the bar, and Bud downs the remains of his drink.

> MARGIE
> Where do we go – my place or yours?

> BUD
> *(peering at his watch)*
> Might as well go to mine – everybody else does.

He leads her through the dark bar toward the entrance. The bartender holds the door open for them as they go out.

DISSOLVE TO:

EXT. BROWNSTONE HOUSE – NIGHT

Bud and Margie come walking down the street. As they reach the house, Bud starts up the steps, but Margie continues along the sidewalk.

> MARGIE
> Poor Mickey – when I think of him all by himself in that jail in Havana –
> *(opening her handbag)*
> – want to see his picture?

> BUD
> *(from steps)*
> Not particularly.

Margie, realizing her mistake, hurries back to join him.

> MARGIE
> He's so cute – five-foot-two – ninety-nine pounds . . . like a little chihuahua.

They pass through the front door into the vestibule.

INT. STAIRCASE – BROWNSTONE HOUSE – NIGHT

Bud and Margie are mounting the stairs toward the apartment.

> MARGIE
> Can I ask you a personal question?

> BUD
> No.

> MARGIE
> You got a girlfriend?

> BUD
> She may be a girl – but she's no friend of mine.

> MARGIE
> Still stuck on her, huh.

> BUD
> Stuck on her! Obviously, you don't know me very well.

> MARGIE
> I don't know you at all.

> BUD
> Permit me – C. C. Baxter – junior executive, Arthur Murray graduate, lover.

> MARGIE
> I'm Mrs MacDougall – Margie to you.

Bud has taken the key out of his pocket, opened the door to his apartment.

> BUD
> This way, Mrs MacDougall.

He ushers her in.

INT. APARTMENT – NIGHT

It is exactly the way we left it. There is no sign of Fran, except for the gloves she dropped on the coffee table earlier. Bud switches on the light, shuts the door.

MARGIE
(*looking around*)

Say, this is Snugsville.

BUD
(*helping her out of her coat*)

Mrs MacDougall, I think it is only fair to warn you that you are now alone with a notorious sexpot.

MARGIE
(*a gleam*)

No kidding.

BUD

Ask anybody around here. As a matter of fact, when it's time for me to go – and I may go just like *that* –
(*snaps his fingers*)
– I have promised my body to the Columbia Medical Center.

MARGIE
(*shuddering deliciously*)

Gee. Sort of gives you goose bumps just to think about it.

BUD

Well, they haven't got me yet, baby. Dig up some ice from the kitchen and let's not waste any time – preliminary-wise.

MARGIE

I'm with you, lover.

She takes the bowl of melted ice Bud has handed her, disappears into the kitchen. As Bud starts to remove his coat, he becomes aware of a scratching noise from the phonograph. He crosses to it, sees that the needle is stuck in the last groove of a long-playing record.

Bud lifts the record off, examines it curiously, then puts it aside and substitutes the cha-cha record. As the music starts, he dances over to the coat-rack beside the door, hangs up his chesterfield and bowler. He turns back into the room, still dancing, suddenly spots Fran's gloves on the coffee table.

He picks up the gloves, looks around for some convenient place to get rid of them. Moving over to the bedroom door, he opens it, tosses the gloves toward the bed inside. He shuts the door, starts to turn away, freezes in a delayed reaction to something he saw inside. He quickly opens the door again, looks.

Sprawled across the bed, on top of the bedspread, is Fran. The light from the bathroom falls across her. She is fully dressed, still in her coat, and apparently asleep.

Bud steps into the bedroom, closing the door behind him, walks over to Fran.

BUD

All right, Miss Kubelik – get up. It's past checking-out time, and the hotel management would appreciate it if you would get the hell out of here.
> (*Fran doesn't stir*)

Look, Miss Kubelik, I used to like you – I used to like you a lot – but it's all over between us – so beat it – O-U-T – out!
> (*no reaction; he puts a hand on her shoulder, shakes her*)

Come on - wake up!

She doesn't respond. But something falls out of her hand, rolls across the bed. Bud picks it up, looks at it – it is his sleeping-pill vial, now uncapped and empty.

> (*a hoarse whisper*)

Oh, my God.

For a second he is paralyzed. Then he drops the vial, grabs Fran, lifts her into a sitting position on the bed, shakes her violently.

Miss Kubelik! *Miss Kubelik!*

Fran's head droops to one side, like a rag doll's. Bud lets go of her, rushes out.

In the living room, the phonograph is still cha-cha-ing away, Bud dashes to the phone, picks it up. Then it occurs to him that he doesn't know whom to call and he hangs up. Out of the kitchen comes Margie, with a bowlful of ice cubes.

MARGIE

I broke a nail trying to get the ice-tray out. You ought to buy yourself a new refrigerator.

Bud, not listening, runs past her to the hall door and out.

> (*calling after him*)
> I didn't mean *right now*.

INT. SECOND FLOOR LANDING – NIGHT

Bud arrives at the door of the Dreyfuss apartment, starts ringing the doorbell and pounding with his fist.

>   BUD
> Dr Dreyfuss! Hey, Doc!

The door opens, and Dr Dreyfuss stands there sleepily, pulling on his beaten bathrobe.

> (*words tumbling over each other*)
> There's a girl in my place – she took some sleeping pills – you better come quick – I can't wake her up.

>   DR DREYFUSS
> Let me get my bag.

He disappears from the doorway.

>   BUD
> Hurry up, Doc.

Bud turns and runs back into his apartment.

INT. APARTMENT – NIGHT

Margie has settled herself comfortably on the couch, and is fixing the drinks. The cha-cha music is still going. Bud comes flying in, heads for the bedroom.

>   MARGIE
> Hey – over here, lover.

Bud stops in his tracks, suddenly aware of her.

> What's all this running around? You're going to wear yourself out.

Bud strides over to her purposefully, yanks her up to her feet.

Not so rough, honey.

BUD

(taking the glass out of her hand)

Good night.

MARGIE

Good night?

BUD

(thrusting the fur coat at her)

The party's over.

MARGIE

What's the matter? Did I do something wrong?

BUD

(easing her toward door)

It's an emergency – see you some other time.

Dr Dreyfuss comes hurrying in, carrying his medical bag. He stops, bewildered by the sound of music and the sight of a wide-awake girl in the apartment.

Not this one –

(pointing to the bedroom)

– in there, Doc.

Dr Dreyfuss proceeds into the bedroom.

MARGIE

Say, what's going on here, anyway?

BUD

Nothing.

(propelling her toward the door)

Just clear out, will you?

MARGIE

(pointing back)

My shoes.

Bud reaches under the coffee table, where she left her shoes, retrieves them.

(*bitterly*)
Some lover *you* are. Some sexpot!

Bud shoves the shoes at her, takes a bill out of his wallet, hands it to her.

BUD
Here – find yourself a phone booth and call your husband in Havana.

MARGIE
You bet I will. And when I tell him how you treated me, he'll push your face in.
      (*he shoves her through the open door*)
You fink!

Bud slams the door shut, starts toward the bedroom. Halfway there, he becomes aware that the cha-cha record is still on. He detours to the phonograph, switches it off, continues into the bedroom.

In the bedroom, the overhead light is on, and Dr Dreyfuss is working on the unconscious Fran. He has removed her coat, and is shining a flashlight into her eyes, examining her pupils. Bud approaches the bed worriedly.

BUD
She going to be all right, Doc?

DR DREYFUSS
How many pills were in that bottle?

BUD
It was half-full – about a dozen or so. You going to have to take her to the hospital?

Dr Dreyfuss ignores him. Out of his medical bag, he takes a stomach tube with a rubber funnel at the end. Then he starts to lift Fran off the bed.

DR DREYFUSS
Help me, will you?

Between them, they get Fran into an upright position.

Into the bathroom.

They half-carry, half-drag Fran's limp form toward the bathroom.

BUD

What are you going to do, Doc?

DR DREYFUSS

Get that stuff out of her stomach – if it isn't too late. You
better put some coffee on – and pray.

Bud starts away as Dr Dreyfuss takes Fran into the bathroom.

*Bud loses no time getting into the kitchen. He fills an aluminium kettle
with water, strikes a match, lights the gas burner, puts the kettle on.
Then he takes a jar of instant coffee and a chipped coffee mug out of the
cupboard, shakes an excessive portion of coffee into the mug, sticks a
spoon in it. He watches the kettle for a moment, mops his brow with a
handkerchief, then starts back toward the bedroom.*

*Bud crosses the bedroom to the half-open door of the bathroom, looks
in anxiously. From inside comes the sounds of a coughing spasm and
running water. Bud turns away, undoes his tie and collar, paces the*

*bedroom floor. Something on the night table attracts his attention –
resting against the base of the lamp is a sealed envelope. Bud picks it
up – on it, in Fran's handwriting, is one word, JEFF. He turns the
letter over in his hand, trying to decide what to do with it.*

*Dr Dreyfuss emerges from the bathroom, carrying a pale, still
unconscious Fran. Bud quickly conceals the suicide note behind his
back.*

DR DREYFUSS

Bring my bag.

*He lugs Fran into the living room. Bud stashes the letter in his back
pocket, picks up the medical bag, follows them.*

*In the living room, Dr Dreyfuss lowers Fran into a chair. Her chin
falls to her chest. Dreyfuss take the bag from Bud, fishes out a
hypodermic.*

Roll up her right sleeve.

*Bud does so. Dr Dreyfuss hands the hypodermic to Bud, searches for a
spot for the injection.*

Nice veins.

He swabs the spot with alcohol, takes the hypodermic back from Bud.

Want to tell me what happened?

BUD

I don't know – I mean – I wasn't here – you see – we had
some words earlier – nothing serious, really – what you might
call a lovers' quarrel –

DR DREYFUSS
(making off-scene injection)

So you went right out and picked yourself up another dame.

BUD

Something like that.

You know, Baxter, you're a real cutie-pie – yes, you are.

Bud just stands there, taking it. Fran stirs slightly, and from her parched lips comes a low moan. Dr Dreyfuss grabs her by the hair, lifts her head up.

If you'd come home half an hour later, you would have had quite a Christmas present.

With his free hand, Dr Dreyfuss slaps Fran viciously across the face. Bud winces. Dreyfuss, still holding Fran by the hair, takes a box of ammonia ampules out of his bag. He crushes one of the ampules in his hands, passes it under her nose. Fran tries to turn her head away. Dreyfuss slaps her again, hard, crushes another ampule, repeats the process.

Bud is watching tensely. From the kitchen comes the whistle of the boiling kettle, but Bud pays no attention.

Get the coffee.

Bud hurries into the kitchen. He turns off the gas, pours the boiling water into the mug with the instant coffee, stirs it. From off, come the sounds of more slapping and some moaning. Bud carries the coffee out.

In the living room, Dr Dreyfuss is working another ammonia ampule under Fran's nose. Her eyes start fluttering. Dreyfuss takes the coffee mug from Bud, forces it between Fran's lips, pours coffee into her mouth. Fran resists instinctively, half the coffee dribbling over her chin and dress, but Dr Dreyfuss keeps at it.

Let's get some air in here. Open the windows.

Bud complies promptly – pulls up the shades, opens the windows wide.

     (putting the empty mug down)
What's her name?

       BUD
Miss Kubelik – Fran.

Fran mutters something.

95

Fran, I'm Dr Dreyfuss – I'm here to help you. You took all those sleeping pills – remember?

> FRAN
> (*mumbling groggily*)

Sleeping pills.

> DR DREYFUSS

That's right, Fran. And I'm a doctor.

> FRAN

Doctor.

> DR DREYFUSS

Dr Dreyfuss.

> FRAN

Dreyfuss.

> DR DREYFUSS
> (*to Bud*)

Get more coffee.

Bud picks up the mug, leaves.

> (*to Fran*)

Tell me again – what's my name?

> FRAN

Dr Dreyfuss.

> DR DREYFUSS

And what happened to you?

> FRAN

I took sleeping pills.

> DR DREYFUSS

Do you know where you are, Fran?

> FRAN
> (*looking around blankly*)

No.

DR DREYFUSS

Yes, you do. Now concentrate.

FRAN

I don't know.

Bud is coming back with the coffee.

DR DREYFUSS
(*pointing to Bud*)

Do you know who this is?

Fran tries to focus.

Look at him.

FRAN

Mr Baxter – nineteenth floor.

BUD

Hello, Miss Kubelik.

DR DREYFUSS
(*to Bud*)

Mister – Miss – such politeness!

BUD
(*to Dr Dreyfuss, discreetly*)

Well – we work in the same building – and we try to keep it
quiet –

FRAN
(*to Bud, puzzled*)

What are you doing here?

*Bud throws Dr Dreyfuss a look, as if to say that Fran's mind still
wasn't functioning properly.*

BUD
(*to Fran*)

Don't you remember? We were at the office party together –

FRAN

Oh, yes – office party – Miss Olsen –

BUD

That's right.
> (*to Dr Dreyfuss; improvising rapidly*)

I told you we had a fight – that's what it was about – Miss Olsen – you know – that other girl you saw –

FRAN
> (*still trying to figure out Bud's presence*)

I don't understand –

BUD

It's not important, Fran – the main thing is that I got here in time – and you're going to be all right –
> (*to Dr Dreyfuss*)

– isn't she, Doc?

FRAN
> (*closing her eyes*)

I'm so tired –

DR DREYFUSS

Here – drink this.

He forces her to swallow some coffee.

FRAN
> (*pushing the mug away*)

Please – just let me sleep.

DR DREYFUSS

You can't sleep.
> (*shaking her*)

Come on, Fran – open your eyes.
> (*to Bud*)

Let's get her walking. We've got to keep her awake for the next couple of hours.

They lift her from the chair, and each draping one of her arms over his shoulder, they start to walk her up and down the room.

DR DREYFUSS
> (*urging Fran on*)

Now walk, Fran. One, two, three, four – one, two, three, four

– that's the idea – left, right, left, right – now we turn – one, two, three, four –

At first, Fran's feet just drag along the floor between them. But gradually, as Dr Dreyfuss' voice continues droning hypnotically, she falls into the rhythm of it, repeating the words after him and putting her weight on her feet.

Left, right, left, right – walk, walk, walk – one, two, three, four – turn – left, right, left, right – now you got it –

DISSOLVE TO:

INT. THE APARTMENT – DAWN

Through the bedroom window comes the first faint light of dawn. Fran has been put to bed by an exhausted Dr Dreyfuss. She is in her slip, and Dreyfuss is just drawing the blanket over her. Her eyes are closed, and she is moaning fitfully. Watching from the doorway is Bud, in shirtsleeves now, weary and dishevelled.

DR DREYFUSS
She'll sleep on and off for the next twenty-four hours. Of course, she'll have a dandy hangover when she wakes up –

BUD
Just as long as she's okay.

DR DREYFUSS
(*massaging his calves*)
These cases are harder on the doctor than on the patient. I ought to charge you by the mile.

They have now moved out into the living room, where the overhead light and the Christmas tree bulbs are still on.

Any of that coffee left?

BUD
Sure.

He goes into the kitchen. Dr Dreyfuss takes a small notebook with a fountain pen clipped to it out of his bag, sinks down on the couch.

DR DREYFUSS
How do you spell her last name?

BUD
(*from kitchen*)
Kubelik – with two k's.

DR DREYFUSS
What's her address?
(*no answer from Bud*)
Where does she live?

Bud appears from the kitchen, stirring the coffee powder in a cup of hot water.

BUD
(*apprehensive*)
Why do you want to know, Doc? You don't have to report this, do you?

DR DREYFUSS
It's regulations.

BUD
(*setting the coffee down*)
She didn't mean it, Doc – it was an accident – she had a little too much to drink and – she didn't know what she was doing – there was no suicide note or anything – believe me, Doc, I'm not thinking about myself –

DR DREYFUSS
(*sipping the hot coffee*)
Aren't you?

BUD
It's just that she's got a family – and there's the people in the office – look, Doc, can't you forget you're a doctor – let's just say you're here as a neighbor –

DR DREYFUSS
(*a long look at Bud*)
Well, as a doctor, I guess I can't prove it *wasn't* an accident.

> (*closes notebook*)

But as your neighbor, I'd like to kick your keester clear
around the block.

> (*indicating coffee*)

Mind if I cool this off?

He uncaps the bottle of Scotch, pours a large slug into his coffee.

BUD

Help yourself.

DR DREYFUSS

> (*taking a big gulp of the spiked coffee*)

I don't know what you did to that girl in there – and don't tell
me – but it was bound to happen, the way you carry on. Live
now, pay later. Diner's Club!

> (*another swig*)

Why don't you grow up, Baxter? Be a *mensch*! You know what
that means?

BUD

I'm not sure.

DR DREYFUSS

A mensch – a human being! So you got off easy this time – so
you were lucky –

BUD

Yeah, wasn't I?

DR DREYFUSS

> (*finishing coffee*)

But you're not out of the woods yet, Baxter – because most of
them try it again!

> (*picks up bag, starts toward door*)

You know where I am if you need me.

*He walks out, closing the door after him. Bud dejectedly turns off the
overhead light, kicks out the plug of the Christmas tree lights, trudges
into the bedroom.*

*Fran is fast asleep. Bud picks up her dress, gets a hanger, drapes the
dress over it, hangs it from the door. An early morning chill has invaded*

*the room, and Bud switches on the electric blanket to keep Fran warm.
Then he slumps into a chair beside the bed, looks at Fran
compassionately. The light on the dial of the electric blanket glows
in the grayish room. Bud just sits there, watching Fran.*

FADE OUT:

FADE IN:

INT. STAIRCASE – BROWNSTONE HOUSE – DAY

*Mrs Lieberman, followed by her dog, is climbing the stairs to Bud's
apartment, puffing asthmatically. She seems quite angry as she arrives
at the door and rings the bell. There is no answer. She starts knocking
impatiently.*

MRS LIEBERMAN

Mr Baxter. Open up already!

*Finally the door opens a crack, and Bud peers out. He looks like a man
who has slept in his clothes – rumpled, bleary-eyed, unshaven.*

BUD

Oh – Mrs Lieberman.

MRS LIEBERMAN.

So who did you think it was – Kris Kringle? What was going
on here last night?

BUD

Last night?

MRS LIEBERMAN

All that marching – tramp, tramp, tramp – you were having
army maneuvers maybe?

BUD

I'm sorry, Mrs Lieberman – and I'll never invite those people
again.

MRS LIEBERMAN

What you get from renting to bachelors. All night I didn't
sleep ten minutes – and I'm sure you woke up Dr Dreyfuss.

BUD

Don't worry about Dr Dreyfuss – I happen to know he was
out on a case.

MRS LIEBERMAN

I'm warning you Mr Baxter – this is a respectable house, not a
honky-tonky.
(*to the dog*)
Come on, Oscar.

*Bud watches her start down the stairs with the dog, withdraws into the
apartment.*

INT. THE APARTMENT – DAY

*Bud closes the door, crosses toward the bedroom, looks inside. Fran is
asleep under the electric blanket, breathing evenly. He tries to shut the
bedroom door, but it won't close completely because Fran's dress, on a
hanger, is hooked over the top. He goes to the phone, picks it up, dials
the operator.*

BUD
(*his voice low*)
Operator, I want White Plains, New York – Mr. J. D.
Sheldrake –
(*an added thought*)
– make it person to person.

INT. LIVING ROOM – SHELDRAKE HOUSE – DAY

*The decor is split-level Early American. There is a huge Christmas tree
and a jumble of presents, open gift boxes, and discarded wrappings.*

*Sheldrake and his two sons, Tommy and Jeff Jr, are squatting on the
floor, testing a Cape Canaveral set the kids got for Christmas.
Sheldrake is in a brand-new dressing-gown, with a manufacturer's tag
still dangling from it, and the boys are in pajamas and astronaut's
helmets. As for the Cape Canaveral set, it is a miniature layout of
block-houses, launching pads, and assorted space-missiles. Tommy has
his finger on the button controlling one of the rockets.*

SHELDRAKE
(*counting down*)
Seven–six–five–four–three–two–one – let her rip!

Tommy presses the button, and a spring sends the rocket toward the ceiling. Just then, the phone in the entrance hall starts ringing.

JEFF JR
I'll get it.

He hurries to the phone.

TOMMY
Hey, Dad – why don't we put a fly in the nose cone and see if we can bring it back alive?

SHELDRAKE
It's a thought.

TOMMY
Maybe we should send up *two* flies – and see if they'll propagate in orbit.

SHELDRAKE
See if they'll *what*?

TOMMY
Propagate – you know, multiply – baby flies?

SHELDRAKE
Oh – oh!

JEFF JR
(*coming back from the phone*)
It's for you, Dad. A Mr Baxter.

SHELDRAKE
(*getting up*)
Baxter?

JEFF JR
Person to person.

Sheldrake heads quickly for the phone.

TOMMY
(*to Jeff Jr*)
Come on – help me round up some flies.

In the entrance hall, Sheldrake picks up the phone, turns his back toward the living room, speaks in a low voice.

SHELDRAKE
Hello? – Yes – what's on your mind, Baxter?

BUD – ON PHONE

BUD
I hate to disturb you, but something came up – it's rather important – and I think it would be a good idea if you could see me – at the apartment – as soon as possible.

SHELDRAKE – ON PHONE
You're not making sense, Baxter. What's this all about?

BUD – ON PHONE
I didn't want to tell you over the phone – but that certain party – you know who I mean – I found her here last night – she had taken an overdose of sleeping pills.

SHELDRAKE – ON PHONE

SHELDRAKE
What?

From the stairway beyond him comes:

MRS SHELDRAKE'S VOICE
What is it, Jeff? Who's on the phone?

Sheldrake turns from the phone. Halfway down the stairs is Mrs Sheldrake, in a quilted house robe.

SHELDRAKE
(*a nice recovery*)
One of our employees had an accident – I don't know why they bother me with these things on Christmas Day.

105

> (*into phone*)
> Yes, Baxter – just how serious is it?

Out of the corner of his eye, he watches Mrs Sheldrake come down the stairs, pass behind him on the way to the living room.

BUD – ON PHONE

> BUD
>
> Well, it was touch and go there for a while – but she's sleeping it off now.

He glances through the half-open door toward the sleeping Fran.

> I thought maybe you'd like to be here when she wakes up.

SHELDRAKE – ON PHONE

> SHELDRAKE
>
> That's impossible.
> (*an apprehensive look toward the living room*)
> You'll have to handle this situation yourself – as a matter of fact, I'm counting on you –

INT. THE APARTMENT – DAY

> BUD
> (*into phone*)
> Yes, sir – I understand.
> (*taking Fran's letter out of his pocket*)
> She left a note – you want me to open it and read it to you?
> (*a beat*)
> Well, it was just a suggestion – no, you don't have to worry about that, Mr Sheldrake – I kept your name out of it – so there'll be no trouble, police-wise or newspaper-wise –

As Bud continues talking on the phone, Fran, in the bedroom, opens her eyes, looks around vaguely, trying to figure out where she is. She sits up in bed, winces, holds her head in her hands – she has a fierce hangover.

> (*into phone*)
> – you see, the doctor, he's a friend of mine – we were very

lucky in that respect – actually, he thinks she's my girl – no, he just jumped to the conclusion – around here, I'm known as quite a ladies' man –

In the bedroom Fran, becoming aware of Bud's voice, crawls out of bed and holding on to the furniture, moves unsteadily toward the living room door.

(*into phone*)
– of course, we're not out of the woods yet – sometimes they try it again – yes sir, I'll do my best – it looks like it'll be a couple of days before she's fully recovered, and I may have a little problem with the landlady –

Behind him, Fran appears in the bedroom doorway, barefooted and in her slip. She leans groggily against the door post, trying to focus on Bud and to concentrate on what he's saying.

(*into phone*)
– all right, Mr Sheldrake, I'll keep her in my apartment as long as I can – any sort of message you want me to give her? – well, I'll think of something – goodbye, Mr Sheldrake.

He hangs up the phone slowly.

FRAN
(*weakly*)
I'm sorry.

Bud turns around, sees her standing there on rubbery legs.

I'm sorry, Mr Baxter.

BUD
Miss Kubelik –
(*hurries toward her*)
– you shouldn't be out of bed.

FRAN
I didn't know – I had no idea this was your apartment –

BUD
(*putting his arm around her*)
Let me help you.

107

He leads her back into the bedroom.

FRAN

I'm so ashamed. Why didn't you just let me die?

BUD

What kind of talk is that?
                    (*he lowers her into the bed*)
So you got a little over-emotional – but you're fine now.

FRAN

(*a groan*)
My head – it feels like a big wad of chewing gum. What time
is it?

BUD

Two o'clock.

FRAN

(*struggling to her feet*)
Where's my dress? I have to go home.

Her knees buckle. Bud catches her.

BUD

You're in no condition to go anywhere – except back to bed.

FRAN

You don't want me here –

BUD

Sure I do. It's always nice to have company for Christmas.

He tries to put her back to bed. Fran resists.

BUD

Miss Kubelik, I'm stronger than you are –

FRAN

I just want to go brush my teeth –

BUD

Oh – of course. I think there's a new toothbrush somewhere.

*He crosses to the bathroom, takes a plaid robe off the hook on the back
of the door, hands it to Fran.*

Here – put this on.

In the bathroom, he finds an unused toothbrush in a plastic container. His eyes fall on his safety razor. With a glance toward the bedroom, he unscrews the razor, removes the blade, drops it in his shirt pocket. Then he empties the blades from the dispenser, puts those in his pocket. Now he notices a bottle of iodine on the medicine shelf, stashes that in another pocket, just as Fran appears in the doorway wearing the robe.

> BUD
> (*handing her the toothbrush*)
> Here. How about some breakfast?

> FRAN
> No – I don't want anything.

> BUD
> I'll fix you some coffee.

He crosses the bedroom, heading for the kitchen, stops.

> Oh – we're all out of coffee – you had quite a lot of it last night –

He thinks for a moment, hurries toward the hall door.

INT. SECOND FLOOR LANDING – DAY

Bud comes out of his apartment, leaving the door half open, heads for the Dreyfuss apartment. He rings the bell, peers down over the banister to make sure Mrs Lieberman isn't snooping around. Mrs Dreyfuss opens the door.

> BUD
> Mrs Dreyfuss, can I borrow some coffee – and maybe an orange and a couple of eggs?

> MRS DREYFUSS
> (*contemptuously*)
> Eggs he asks me for. Oranges. What you need is a good horse-whipping.

BUD

Ma'am?

MRS DREYFUSS

From me the doctor has no secrets. Poor girl – how could you do a thing like that?

BUD

I didn't really do anything – honest – I mean, you take a girl out a couple of times a week – just for laughs – and right away she thinks you're serious – marriage-wise.

MRS DREYFUSS

Big shot! For you, I wouldn't lift a finger – but for her, I'll fix a little something to eat.

She slams the door in his face. Bud starts back to his apartment.

INT. THE APARTMENT – DAY

Fran enters shakily from the bedroom, looks around for the phone, locates it, picks it up. As she starts dialling, Bud comes in from the hall.

BUD

Who are you calling, Miss Kubelik?

FRAN

My sister – she'll want to know what happened to me.

BUD
(*alarmed*)
Wait a minute – let's talk this over first.
(*hurries up to her, takes the receiver away*)
Just what are you going to tell her?

FRAN

Well, I haven't figured it out, exactly.

BUD

You better figure it out – exactly. Suppose she asks you why you didn't come home last night?

FRAN

I'll tell her I spent the night with a friend.

III

                    BUD

Who?

                    FRAN

Someone from the office.

                    BUD

And where are you now?

                    FRAN

In his apartment.

                    BUD

His apartment?

                    FRAN

I mean – *her* apartment.

                    BUD

What's your friend's name?

                    FRAN

Baxter.

                    BUD

What's her first name?

                    FRAN

Miss.

            (*impressed with her own cleverness*)

                    BUD

When are you coming home?

                    FRAN

As soon as I can walk.

                    BUD

Something wrong with your legs?

                    FRAN

No – it's my stomach.

                    BUD

Your stomach?

FRAN

They had to pump it out.

BUD
(*hanging up the phone*)
Miss Kubelik, I don't think you ought to call anybody – not
till that chewing gum is out of your head.
(*leads her into bedroom*)

FRAN

But they'll be worried about me – my brother-in-law may be
calling the police –

BUD

That's why we have to be careful – we don't want to involve
anybody – after all, Mr Sheldrake is a married man –

FRAN

Thanks for reminding me.

She pulls away from him, starts to get into bed.

BUD
(*contritely*)
I didn't mean it that way – I was just talking to him on the
phone – he's very concerned about you.

FRAN

He doesn't give a damn about me.

BUD

Oh, you're wrong. He told me –

FRAN

He's a liar. But that's not the worst part of it – the worst part
is – I still love him.

The doorbell rings.

BUD

Must be Mrs Dreyfuss –
(*starts into living room*)
– remember the doctor – from last night – that's his wife.

He opens the hall door. Mrs Dreyfuss brushes past him with a tray full of food.

> MRS DREYFUSS
>
> So where is the victim?
> > (*Bud indicates the bedroom*)
>
> Max the Knife!

She sweeps into the bedroom, Bud tagging along.

> MRS DREYFUSS
> > (*to Fran*)
>
> Nu, little lady, how are we feeling today?

> FRAN
>
> I don't know – kind of dizzy.

> MRS DREYFUSS
>
> Here. The best thing for dizzy is a little noodle soup with chicken – white meat – and a glass tea.

She sets the tray down on Fran's lap.

> FRAN
>
> Thank you. I'm really not hungry.

> MRS DREYFUSS
>
> Go ahead! Eat! Enjoy!

She hands her the soup spoon, turns to Bud.

> MRS DREYFUSS
>
> You wouldn't have such a thing as a napkin, would you?

> BUD
>
> Well, I have some paper towels –

> MRS DREYFUSS
>
> Beatnik! Go to my kitchen – third drawer, under the good silver, there is napkins.

> BUD
>
> Yes, Mrs Dreyfuss.

He starts out with a worried backward glance toward the two. Fran is just sitting there, the spoon in her hand, not touching the soup.

MRS DREYFUSS

So what are you waiting for – a singing commercial?

FRAN

I can't eat.

Mrs Dreyfuss takes the spoon from her, starts to feed her.

MRS DREYFUSS

You *must* eat – and you must get healthy – and you must forget him. Such a fine boy he seemed when he first moved in here – clean and cut – a regular Ivy Leaguer. Turns out he is King Farouk. Mit the drinking – mit the cha-cha – mit the no napkins. A girl like you, for the rest of your life you want to cry in your noodle soup? Who needs it! You listen to me, you find yourself a nice, substantial man – a widower maybe – and settle down – instead of nashing all those sleeping pills – for what, for whom? – for some Good Time Charlie?
> (*sees Bud approaching with napkin*)

Sssh!

BUD
> (*gaily*)

One napkin, coming up.
> (*hands it to Fran*)

I wish we had some champagne to wrap it around.

MRS DREYFUSS
> (*to Fran*)

What did I tell you?

BUD
> (*uncomfortable*)

Look, Mrs Dreyfuss, you don't have to wait around. I'll wash the dishes and –

MRS DREYFUSS

You wash 'em, you break 'em. I'll come back for them later.
> (*to Fran*)

If he makes trouble, give me a yell.

She exits.

FRAN

She doesn't seem to like you very much.

BUD

Oh, I don't mind. As a matter of fact, I'm sort of flattered –
that anybody should think a girl like you – would do a thing
like this – over a guy like me.

FRAN
(*glancing at night table*)
Oh. Did you find something here – an envelope – ?

BUD

Yes, I've got it.
(*takes envelope out of back pocket*)
Don't you think we'd better destroy it? So it won't fall into
the wrong hands – ?

FRAN

Open it.

Bud tears open the envelope, takes out Sheldrake's hundred dollars.

BUD

There's nothing here but a hundred dollar bill.

FRAN

That's right. Will you see that Mr Sheldrake gets it?

BUD
(*shrugging*)

Sure.

He puts the money in his pocket.

FRAN
(*holding out tray*)
Here – take this, will you?

Bud relieves her of the tray, sets it down.

BUD

You want me to move the television set in here?

(Fran shakes her head)
You play gin rummy?

FRAN

I'm not very good at it.

BUD

I am. Let me get the cards.

FRAN

You don't have to entertain me.

Bud opens the bureau drawer, takes out a deck of cards, a score pad, and a pencil.

BUD

Nothing I'd like better – you know togetherness. Guess what I did last Christmas. Had an early dinner at the automat, then went to the zoo, then I came home and cleaned up after Mr Eichelberger – he had a little eggnog party here. I'm way ahead this year.

He pulls a chair up to the bed, starts to shuffle the cards.

Three across, spades double, high deals.
(they cut)
Eight – ten.
(he starts to deal)

FRAN
(pensively)
I think I'm going to give it all up.

BUD

Give what up?

FRAN

Why do people have to love people, anyway?

BUD

Yeah – I know what you mean.
(flips over down card)
Queen.

FRAN

I don't want it.

BUD

Pick a card.

She does, and they start playing.

FRAN

What do you call it when somebody keeps getting smashed up in automobile accidents?

BUD

A bad insurance risk?

FRAN
(*nodding*)

That's me with men. I've been jinxed from the word go – first time I was ever kissed was in a cemetery.

BUD

A cemetery?

FRAN

I was fifteen – we used to go there to smoke. His name was George – he threw me over for a drum majorette.

BUD

Gin.

He spreads his hand. Fran lays her cards down, and Bud adds them up.

Thirty-six and twenty-five – that's sixty-one and two boxes.
(*enters score on pad*)

FRAN

I just have this talent for falling in love with the wrong guy in the wrong place at the wrong time.

BUD
(*shuffling*)

How many guys were there?

FRAN
(holding up four fingers)
Three. The last one was manager of a finance company, back
home in Pittsburgh – they found a little shortage in his
accounts, but he asked me to wait for him – he'll be out in
1965.

BUD
(pushing the deck toward her)
Cut.

FRAN
(she does, and he starts dealing)
So I came to New York and moved in with my sister and her
husband – he drives a cab. They sent me to secretarial school,
and I applied for a job with Consolidated – but I flunked the
typing test –

BUD
Too slow?

FRAN
Oh, I can type up a storm, but I can't spell. So they gave me a
pair of white gloves and stuck me in an elevator – that's how I
met Jeff –
(her eyes mist up, and she puts her cards down)
Oh, God, I'm so fouled up. What am I going to do now?

BUD
You better win a hand – you're on a blitz.

FRAN
Was he really upset when you told him?

BUD
Mr Sheldrake? Oh, yes. Very.

FRAN
Maybe he *does* love me – only he doesn't have the nerve to tell
his wife.

BUD
I'm sure that's the explanation.

FRAN

You really think so?

BUD

No doubt about it.

FRAN
(*a thoughtful beat, then*)
Can I have that pad and the pencil?

BUD
(*handing her score pad and pencil*)
What for?

FRAN

I'm going to write a letter to *Mrs* Sheldrake.

BUD

You *are*?

FRAN

As one woman to another – I'm sure she'll understand –

BUD

Miss Kubelik, I don't think that's such a good idea.

He gently takes the pad and pencil away from her.

FRAN

Why not?

BUD

Well, for one thing, you can't spell. And secondly – if you did
something like that – you'd hate yourself.

FRAN
(*fighting back tears*)
I don't like myself very much anyway.

BUD

Pick up your cards and let's go.

FRAN

Do I have to?

BUD

You bet. I got a terrific hand.

Fran, her eyes drooping sleepily, picks up her cards, makes a discard.

You sure you want to throw that card?

FRAN

Sure.

BUD

Gin.

He removes the cards from her hand, starts to add them up.

Fifty-two and twenty-five – that's seventy-seven – spades is double – a hundred and fifty-four – and four boxes – you're blitzed in two games.

He enters the score on the pad. As he starts to shuffle again, he notices that Fran has slid down on the pillow, and that her eyes are closed – she is asleep.

Bud rises, adjusts the blanket over her. He stands there looking at her for a moment, runs his hand over his chin. Realizing he needs a shave, he crosses to the bathroom.

In the bathroom, Bud washes his face, squirts some shaving cream into his hand, starts to apply it.

EXT. BROWNSTONE HOUSE – DAY

A Volkswagen draws up to the curb in front of the house. Kirkeby gets out on the street side, Sylvia squeezes herself out through the other door. Kirkeby raises the front hood of the Volkswagen, reaches into the luggage compartment, takes out a cardboard bucket with a bottle of champagne on ice. Together, he and Sylvia start up the steps of the house, Sylvia already cha-cha-ing in anticipation.

INT. APARTMENT – DAY

In the bathroom, Bud has just finished lathering his face when the doorbell rings. He starts into the bedroom.

                              BUD
                    (*muttering to himself*)
        All right – all right, Mrs Dreyfuss.

*He glances at the sleeping Fran, picks up the tray, carries it into the
living room, pulling the bedroom door closed behind him. But it doesn't
shut completely, because of Fran's dress hooked over the top.*

*Bud crosses to the hall door, opens it. Outside are Kirkeby, with the
champagne bucket, and Sylvia.*

                            KIRKEBY
        Hi, Baxter.

                              BUD
                      (*blocking the door*)
        What do you want?

                            KIRKEBY
        What do I – ?
                          (*to Sylvia*)
        Just a minute.

He pushes his way into the apartment past Bud.

                              BUD
        You can't come in.

                            KIRKEBY
                  (*closing the door behind him*)
        What's the matter with you, Buddy-boy? I made a reservation
        for four o'clock, remember?

                              BUD
        Look, you can't stay here. Just take your champagne and go.

                            KIRKEBY
        Baxter, I don't want to pull rank on you – but I told the lady
        it was all set – you want to make a liar out of me?

                              BUD
        Are you going to leave, Mr Kirkeby, or do I have to throw
        you out?

                              122

As Bud spins him around, Kirkeby notices the dress on the bedroom door.

KIRKEBY
Buddy-boy, why didn't you say so?
                    (*indicating dress*)
You got yourself a little playmate, huh?

BUD
Now will you get out?

INT. SECOND FLOOR LANDING – DAY

Outside the door of Bud's apartment, Sylvia is cha-cha-ing impatiently. Up the stairs comes Dr Dreyfuss, in his overcoat and carrying his medical bag.

SYLVIA
(*knocking on the door*)
Hey, come on, what are we waiting for? Open up, will you?

She continues cha-cha-ing. Dr Dreyfuss has unlocked the door to his apartment, and is watching Sylvia, appalled by the fact that Baxter seems to be at it again. He starts inside.

DR DREYFUSS
(*calling*)
Mildred – !

He shuts the door behind him.

SYLVIA
(*knocking on Baxter's door*)
What's holding things up?

INT. APARTMENT – DAY

Kirkeby looks toward the door in response to Sylvia's knocking.

KIRKEBY
Say, why don't we have ourselves a party – the four of us?

BUD
No!

He forces Kirkeby toward the hall door. Kirkeby, glancing past him through the partly open door of the bedroom, catches sight of Fran asleep in bed.

> KIRKEBY
> *(grinning smugly)*
> Well, I don't blame you. So you hit the jackpot, eh kid – I mean, Kubelik-wise?

Bud opens the door, gestures him out.

> Don't worry. I won't say a word to anybody.

INT. SECOND FLOOR LANDING – DAY

Kirkeby comes backing out of the door of Bud's apartment, minus the champagne bucket.

> KIRKEBY
> Stay with it, Buddy-boy!

Bud shuts the door on him.

> Come on, Sylvia.

> SYLVIA
> What gives?

> KIRKEBY
> A little mixup in signals. Let's go.

> SYLVIA
> Go where?

> KIRKEBY
> *(leading her toward stairs)*
> What's your mother doing this afternoon?

> SYLVIA
> She's home – stuffing a turkey.

> KIRKEBY
> Why don't we send her to a movie – like *Ben-Hur*?

> SYLVIA
> That's fine. But what are we going to do about Grandma and

Uncle Herman and Aunt Sophie and my two nieces –

Bud comes into the bedroom. As he heads for the bathroom, Fran stirs slightly, opens her eyes.

FRAN

Who was that?

BUD

Just somebody delivering a bottle of champagne. Like some?

FRAN
(*shaking her head*)
Would you mind opening the window?

She turns off the electric blanket as Bud crosses to the window, pushes it up. Then a thought strikes him, and he looks at Fran suspiciously.

BUD

Now don't go getting any ideas, Miss Kubelik.

FRAN

I just want some fresh air.

BUD

It's only one story down – the best you can do is break a leg.

FRAN

So they'll shoot me – like a horse.

BUD
(*approaching the bed*)
Please, Miss Kubelik, you got to promise me you won't do anything foolish.

FRAN

Who'd care?

BUD

I would.

FRAN
(*sleepily*)
Why can't I ever fall in love with somebody nice like you?

BUD
(*ruefully*)
Yeah. Well – that's the way it crumbles, cookie-wise. Go to sleep.

Fran closes her eyes. Bud returns to the bathroom, picks up his razor, starts to shave. But something seems to be wrong with the razor – and unscrewing it, he realizes that there is no blade. Sheepishly, he takes out the blade he hid in his shirt pocket, inserts it in his razor, screws it shut. Then he resumes shaving.

FADE OUT:

FADE IN:

INT. SHELDRAKE'S ANTEROOM – DAY

It is the morning after Christmas, and Miss Olsen and the other girls are just settling down to work. Sheldrake, in hat and coat, approaches from the elevators, comes through the glass doors.

SECRETARIES
(*ad lib*)
Good morning, Mr Sheldrake.

SHELDRAKE
(*ignoring them*)
Miss Olsen, will you come into my office, please?

He strides into the inner office. Miss Olsen picks up her stenographic pad, follows him in.

INT. SHELDRAKE'S OFFICE – DAY

Sheldrake is removing his hat and coat as Miss Olsen comes in, shuts the door behind her.

MISS OLSEN
Did you have a nice Christmas?

SHELDRAKE

Lovely. You were a big help.

MISS OLSEN

Me?

SHELDRAKE

Thank you for giving that little pep talk to Miss Kubelik at the
office party.

MISS OLSEN
(*dropping her business-like mask*)
I'm sorry, Jeff. You know I could never hold my liquor –

SHELDRAKE

But I thought you could hold your tongue.

MISS OLSEN

It won't happen again.

SHELDRAKE

You bet it won't. I'll arrange for you to get a month's
severance pay –

(*she looks at him, uncomprehending*)
That's right, Miss Olsen. I'm letting you go.

MISS OLSEN
(*quietly*)
You let me go four years ago, Jeff. Only you were cruel
enough to make me sit out there and watch the new models
pass by.

SHELDRAKE
I'd appreciate it if you'd be out of here as soon as you can.

MISS OLSEN
(*formal again*)
Yes, Mr Sheldrake.

*She turns and walks out of the office, shutting the door. Sheldrake looks
after her for a moment, then goes to his desk, picks up the phone, dials
the operator.*

SHELDRAKE
(*into phone*)
This is Mr Sheldrake. I'd like Mr Baxter's home telephone
number – that's C. C. Baxter, in Ordinary Premium
Accounting –

INT. SHELDRAKE'S ANTEROOM – DAY

*Miss Olsen has put on her coat, and is going through her desk drawers,
cleaning out her personal belongings – nail polish, emery boards, an
extra pair of glasses, etc. As she stows them away in her handbag, one of
the buttons on the telephone lights up. Miss Olsen hesitates for a second,
then with a quick look around, she pushes the button down, carefully
picks up the receiver, listens in.*

INT. SHELDRAKE'S OFFICE – DAY

*Sheldrake is dialing the last two digits of a telephone number. After a
moment, someone answers.*

SHELDRAKE
Hello, Baxter? Jeff Sheldrake. Can you talk?

INT. THE APARTMENT – DAY

Bud, wearing slacks, a shirt open at the neck, and a cardigan sweater, is at the phone.

A pillow and a blanket on the living room couch indicate where he spent the night.

> BUD
> (*looking off*)
> Yes, she's in the shower – she's coming along fine, considering.

SHELDRAKE – ON PHONE

> SHELDRAKE
> Good. Is there anything you need – money – ?

BUD – ON PHONE

> BUD
> No, thank you, Mr Sheldrake. As a matter of fact, I've got some money for you – a hundred dollars –

SHELDRAKE – ON PHONE

> SHELDRAKE
> Oh.
> (*a beat*)
> Well, if there's anything I can do for you –

BUD – ON PHONE

> BUD
> For me? I don't think so. But I was hoping maybe you could do something for *her* –

SHELDRAKE – ON PHONE

> SHELDRAKE
> Like what? Put yourself in my place, Baxter – how can I help her – my hands are tied –

INT. APARTMENT – DAY

Fran now appears in the bedroom, wearing the plaid robe, and towelling her damp hair.

> BUD
> (*into phone*)
> Well, at least you can talk to her – let me put her on – and please be gentle –

He puts the receiver down, crosses toward the bedroom door.

> There's a call for you –

> FRAN
> (*approaching*)
> For me?

> BUD
> – Mr Sheldrake.

> FRAN
> I don't want to talk to him.

> BUD
> I think you should. I have to run down to the grocery anyway – all that's left around here is one frozen pizza –
> (*takes raincoat and old hat from hanger*)
> I'll be right back – okay?

Fran nods, watches him go out. Then she glances toward the phone, which is off the hook. Reluctantly she advances toward it, picks it up.

> FRAN
> (*into phone*)
> Hello, Jeff.
> (*a long beat*)
> Yes, I'm all right.

SHELDRAKE – ON PHONE

> SHELDRAKE
> Fran, why did you do it? It's so childish – and it never solves anything – I ought to be very angry with you, scaring me like

that – but let's forget the whole thing – pretend it never happened – what do you say, Fran?

>   (*no answer*)

Fran –

INT. SHELDRAKE'S ANTEROOM

Miss Olsen, glued to the phone, is listening intently.

SHELDRAKE – ON PHONE

>   SHELDRAKE

Are you there, Fran?

FRAN – ON PHONE

>   FRAN

Of course I'm not here – because the whole thing never happened – I never took those pills – I never loved you – we never even met – isn't that the way you want it?

SHELDRAKE – ON PHONE

>   SHELDRAKE

There you go again – you know I didn't mean it that way, Fran. Just get well – do what the nurse tells you – I mean Baxter – and I'll see you as soon as I can. Bye, Fran.

>   (*hangs up*)

INT. SHELDRAKE'S ANTEROOM – DAY

Miss Olsen hangs up the phone, sits there for a moment, weighing what she has overheard. Then she makes a decision, picks up the phone again, dials a number. As she waits for an answer, she glances toward Sheldrake's office.

>   MISS OLSEN
>   (*into phone*)

Hello, Mrs Sheldrake? This is Miss Olsen – fine, thank you – Mrs Sheldrake, I was wondering if we could have lunch together? – Well, I don't know how important it is, but I think

you might find it educational – It concerns your husband –
All right, one o'clock, at Longchamp's, Madison and 59th.

*She looks up as the door to the inner office opens and Sheldrake comes
out. He stops when he sees that Miss Olsen is still there.*

(*hanging up phone*)
Don't worry, I'm on my way.
(*she rises*)
I was just making a personal call.

She opens her handbag, takes out a coin, puts it down on the desk.

Here's a dime.

*She marches out through the glass doors toward the elevators as
Sheldrake stands there, watching her.*

DISSOLVE TO:

EXT. BROWNSTONE HOUSE – DAY

*Bud comes down the street, carrying a large brown-paper bag
overflowing with groceries. He goes up the steps of the house and
through the front door.*

INT. STAIRCASE AND SECOND FLOOR LANDING – DAY

*As Bud starts up the stairs, with the groceries, Mrs Lieberman comes
hurrying down toward him.*

MRS LIEBERMAN
(*breathlessly*)
Oh, Mr Baxter – I'm glad you're here – I was just going to get
the pass-key.

BUD
What for?

MRS LIEBERMAN
I thought I smelled gas coming from your apartment.

BUD
Gas?

132

He races up the stairs two at a time, fumbling frantically for his key. Reaching the door of his apartment, he unlocks it, dashes in.

INT. THE APARTMENT – DAY

Bud comes bursting through the door. The living room is empty, and the bedclothes have been removed from the couch.

> BUD
> *(calling)*

Miss Kubelik!

He dumps the bag of groceries on a table, rushes into the kitchen. The burner has been turned on under the kettle, but there is no flame, and gas is hissing from the vents. Bud snaps it off, starts out again.

Miss Kubelik!

Meanwhile Fran has appeared from the bathroom, and is approaching the bedroom door. She is still in her robe, and is holding a double sock-stretcher with one of Bud's socks on it. Bud, rounding the corner from the kitchen at full speed, collides with Fran in the bedroom doorway. He grabs her arm with obvious relief.

Are you all right?

> FRAN

Sure.

> *(sniffs)*

What's that funny smell?

> BUD

Gas.

> *(indicating kitchen)*

Didn't you turn it on?

> FRAN

Yes. I was boiling some water to get the coffee stains out of my dress.

> BUD
> *(accusingly)*

You turned it on – but you didn't *light* it.

133

FRAN

Are you supposed to?

BUD

In *this* house, you're supposed to.

FRAN

Oh.

Bud starts to take off his hat and coat, notices the sock-stretcher in her hand.

BUD

What are you doing with that?

FRAN

I was washing my stockings, so I decided I might as well do your socks.

BUD

Thank you.

FRAN

It's very curious – I could only find three and a half pair.

BUD

Well, things are a little disorganized around here.

He carries the bag of groceries into the kitchen, Fran trailing after him. During the following, he removes the contents of the bag – bread, eggs, bacon, spaghetti, ground round, frankfurters, and assorted canned goods – sets them out on the drainboard.

FRAN

I'd say. What's a tennis racquet doing in the kitchen?

She produces the racquet from behind the stove.

BUD

Tennis racquet? Oh, I remember – I was cooking myself an Italian dinner.
(*Fran looks at him oddly*)
I used it to strain the spaghetti.

FRAN
(*thinking it over*)

Why not?

BUD

As a matter of fact, I'm a pretty good cook – but I'm a lousy housekeeper.

FRAN

Yes, you are.
(*indicating the living room*)
When I was straightening up the couch, you know what I found? Six hairpins, a lipstick, a pair of false eyelashes, and a swizzle stick from the Stork Club.

BUD
(*shrugging*)
It's just that I'm the kind of guy who can't say no – I don't mean to *girls* – I mean –

FRAN

You mean to someone like Mr Sheldrake.

BUD

I guess so.

FRAN

I know so. He's a taker.

BUD

A what?

FRAN

Some people take, some people get took – and they know they're getting took – and there's nothing they can do about it.

BUD

I wouldn't say that –
(*trying to change the subject*)
What would you like to have for dinner? There's onion soup and canned asparagus –

I really ought to be getting home. My family will be flipping
by now.

She starts into the living room. Bud follows her.

BUD

You can't leave yet. The doctor says it takes forty-eight hours
to get the stuff out of your system.

FRAN
(*wistfully*)

I wonder how long it takes to get someone you're stuck on
out of your system? If they'd only invent some kind of a pump
for that –

She sits on the arm of a chair.

BUD

I know how you feel, Miss Kubelik. You think it's the end of
the world – but it's not, really. I went through exactly the
same thing myself.

FRAN

You did?

BUD

Well, maybe not *exactly* – I tried to do it with a gun.

FRAN

Over a girl?

BUD

Worse than that – she was the wife of my best friend – and I
was mad for her. But I knew it was hopeless – so I decided to
end it all. I went to a pawnshop and bought a forty-five
automatic and drove up to Eden Park – do you know
Cincinnati?

FRAN

No, I don't.

BUD

Anyway, I parked the car and loaded the gun – well, you read

in the papers all the time that people shoot themselves, but believe me, it's not that easy – I mean, how do you do it? – here, or here, or here –
(*with cocked finger, he points to his temple, mouth and chest*)
– you know where I finally shot myself?

FRAN

Where?

BUD
(*indicating kneecap*)

Here.

FRAN

In the knee?

BUD

Uh-huh. While I was sitting there, trying to make my mind up, a cop stuck his head in the car, because I was illegally parked – so I started to hide the gun under the seat and it went off – pow!

FRAN
(*laughing*)

That's terrible.

BUD

Yeah. Took me a year before I could bend my knee – but I got over the girl in three weeks. She still lives in Cincinnati, has four kids, gained twenty pounds – sends me a fruit cake every Christmas.

FRAN
(*suddenly suspicious*)

Are you just making that up to make me feel better?

BUD

Of course not. Here's the fruit cake.
(*shows it to her under Christmas tree*)
And you want to see my knee?

137

(starts to raise pant-leg)

FRAN

No, thanks. The fellows in the office may get the wrong idea how I found out.

BUD

So let 'em. Look, I'm going to cook dinner for us. We'll have the fruit cake for dessert. You just sit there and rest. You've done enough for one day.

FRAN
(smiling)

Yes, nurse.

Bud starts happily into the kitchen.

DISSOLVE TO:

INT. LOBBY INSURANCE BUILDING – DAY

It is mid-afternoon, and traffic is light. A yellow cab has pulled up in front of the entrance, and the driver, a stockily-built young man in a leather jacket and cap, gets out and comes through the revolving doors into the lobby. His name is Karl Matuschka, and he is Fran's brother-in-law. As he cases the elevators, the starter comes up to him.

ELEVATOR STARTER

Can I help you?

MATUSCHKA

I'm looking for one of the elevator girls – Miss Kubelik.

ELEVATOR STARTER

So am I. She didn't report in this morning.

MATUSCHKA

She didn't. Where can I get some information – who's in charge here?

ELEVATOR STARTER

That comes under General Office Administration. See Mr Dobisch, twenty-first floor.

Thanks.

He steps into an elevator, the doors of which are just closing.

INT. DOBISCH'S OFFICE – DAY

Dobisch is sitting behind his desk, lighting a cigar. Kirkeby, who has dropped in for a little visit, is perched on the edge of the desk.

KIRKEBY

– so yesterday afternoon I take Sylvia up to the apartment, and guess who he's got stashed away in the bedroom?

DOBISCH

Who?

KIRKEBY

Kubelik.

DOBISCH

No kidding. Buddy-boy and Kubelik having themselves a little toot!

KIRKEBY

Toot? It's more like a lost weekend. Neither of them showed up for work today.

DOBISCH

AWOL?

KIRKEBY

What gripes me is the two of them were guzzling my champagne while Sylvia and I wound up at the Guggenheim Museum.

The glass door opens and Matuschka comes in.

MATUSCHKA

Mr Dobisch?

DOBISCH

Yeah.

MATUSCHKA

My name is Karl Matuschka – my sister-in-law, she runs one
of the elevators here – Fran Kubelik.

KIRKEBY
(*exchanging a glance with Dobisch*)
Miss Kubelik?

MATUSCHKA

You know her?

DOBISCH

Of course. There may be a lot of employees here – but we're
one big happy family.

MATUSCHKA

Well, she lives with us – and my wife, she's getting a little
nervous – on account of Fran hasn't been home for two days.

KIRKEBY
(*another look at Dobisch*)
That so.

MATUSCHKA

Anyway, we was wondering if somebody in the office would
know what happened to her.

DOBISCH
(*to Kirkeby*)
What do you think, Al? Can we help the man?

KIRKEBY
(*after a pregnant pause*)
Why not? We don't owe Buddy-boy anything.

DOBISCH

Yeah. What's Buddy-boy done for us lately?

MATUSCHKA
(*scowling*)
Who is Buddy-boy?

DISSOLVE TO:

INT. THE APARTMENT – EVENING

Buddy-boy is bending over a hot stove, preparing an Italian dinner. He takes a saucepan of spaghetti off the fire, and picking up the tennis racquet with the other hand, pours the spaghetti on top of the racquet strings. Then he turns on the faucet, runs water over the spaghetti. With the combined technique of Brillat-Savarin and Pancho Gonzales, he gently agitates the racquet, letting the water drain off the spaghetti. As he works, he hums a theme from Tchaikovsky's Italian Capriccio.

Fran walks in, still in her robe.

> FRAN
> Are we dressing for dinner?

> BUD
> No – just come as you are.

> FRAN
> *(watching him)*
> Say, you're pretty good with that racquet.

> BUD
> You ought to see my backhand.
> *(dumping spaghetti into platter)*
> And wait till I serve the meatballs.
> *(demonstrates)*

> FRAN
> Shall I light the candles?

> BUD
> It's a must – gracious-living-wise.

As Fran starts into the living room, Bud begins to ladle meat sauce onto the spaghetti, humming operatically.

In the living room, the small table has been set for two, and prominent on it is the champagne bottle that Mr Kirkeby left behind, still in its cardboard bucket, but freshly iced. As Fran lights the candles, she notices the napkins on the table, peels a price tag off the corner of one of them.

141

FRAN

I see you bought some napkins.

BUD

Might as well go all the way.

He carries the platter of spaghetti and meat sauce in from the kitchen, sets it on the table, sprinkles some cheese on it. Then he crosses to the coffee table, where a full martini pitcher stands in readiness, fills a couple of glasses. Fran seats herself at the table.

You know, I used to live like Robinson Crusoe – shipwrecked among eight million people. Then one day I saw a footprint in the sand – and there you were –
                    (*hands her martini*)
It's a wonderful thing – dinner for two.

FRAN

You usually eat alone?

BUD

Oh, no. Sometimes I have dinner with Ed Sullivan,

sometimes with Dinah Shore or Perry Como – the other night
I had dinner with Mae West – of course, she was much
younger then.

(*toasting*)

Cheers.

They drink.

You know what we're going to do after dinner?

FRAN

The dishes?

BUD

I mean, after that?

FRAN

What?

BUD

You don't have to if you don't want to –

FRAN

I don't?

BUD

We're going to finish that gin game.

FRAN

Oh.

BUD

So I want you to keep a clear head.

*The doorbell rings. Carrying his martini glass, Bud crosses to the door,
starts to open it.*

Because I don't want to take advantage of you – the way I did
yesterday in bed.

*By now the door is open, and Bud is speaking to Fran over his shoulder.
He turns, finds himself face to face with Karl Matuschka, who is
standing grimly in the doorway.*

MATUSCHKA

Baxter?

BUD

Yes?

Matuschka shoves him roughly aside, strides past him toward Fran, who has risen to her feet.

MATUSCHKA

What's with you, Fran – did you forget where you live?

FRAN
(*to Bud*)

This is my brother-in-law, Karl Matuschka.

BUD
(*friendly*)

How do you do, Mr Matuschka?

MATUSCHKA
(*pushing Bud away; to Fran*)

Okay, get your clothes on. I got the cab downstairs.

BUD

Now, wait a minute. I know what you're thinking – but it's not as bad as it looks –

MATUSCHKA
(*shoving him away*)

It's none of my business what you do, Fran – you're over twenty-one – but your sister happens to think you're a lady.

BUD

All we were going to do is eat and wash the dishes –

MATUSCHKA
(*grabbing him*)

Look, Buddy-boy – if there wasn't a lady present, I'd clobber you.

FRAN
(*separating them*)

All right, Karl – I'll get dressed.

She exits into the bedroom, removing her dress from the door, and
closing it. Matuschka leans against the wall beside the hall door, eyeing
Bud truculently. Bud raises a finger to remonstrate with him – then
breaks into a nervous, ingratiating smile.

BUD

Care for a martini? Champagne?
> (*Matuschka continues glaring at him*)
How about a little spaghetti with meat sauce? Made it myself.
> (*Matuschka just scowls*)
Your sister-in-law sure is terrific –
> (*realizes his mistake; switching abruptly*)
Must be murder driving a cab in New York – I mean, with all
that cross-town traffic –

He gestures with the martini glass, spilling the contents over his
shirtfront. Through the partly open hall door, Dr Dreyfuss sticks his
head in.

DR DREYFUSS

Hi, Baxter.

He steps into the apartment, passing Matuschka without seeing him.

How's the patient?

BUD
> (*quickly*)

Oh, I'm fine, Doc.

DR DREYFUSS

Not you – Miss Kubelik.

MATSCHUKA
> (*stepping forward*)

What's the matter with Miss Kubelik?

BUD

Oh, this is Mr Matuschka – he's Miss Kubelik's – he's got a
cab downstairs –

MATUSCHKA
> (*to Dreyfuss*)

Fran been sick or something?

145

Dr Dreyfuss looks at Bud.

BUD

No, no – just had a little accident.

MATUSCHKA
(to Dreyfuss)

What does he mean, accident?

DR DREYFUSS

Well, these things happen all the time –

MATUSCHKA

What things?
(grabbing Dreyfuss)
Say, what kind of doctor are you, anyway?

BUD
(hastily)

Oh, not that kind. He just gave her a shot and pumped her
stomach out –

*Behind them, the bedroom door has opened, and Fran comes out,
wearing her coat over her dress.*

MATUSCHKA

What for?

FRAN
(coming up)

Because I took some sleeping pills. But I'm all right now – so
let's go.

MATUSCHKA

Why did you take sleeping pills?

BUD
(promptly)

On account of me.

MATUSCHKA
(whirling on him)

You?

Who else?

Matuschka lashes out with a left to Bud's jaw, and while he is off balance, catches him with a right to the eye. Bud falls back against the Christmas tree, which topples with a crash. Fran pulls Matuschka away from him.

FRAN

Leave him alone, Karl.

She kneels beside Bud.

(*tenderly*)
You fool – you damn fool.

MATUSCHKA

Come on, Fran.

FRAN

Goodbye, Mr Baxter.

She kisses him on the cheek, rises, starts toward the door.

Goodbye, Doctor.

She follows Matuschka out. Bud looks after her, starry-eyed.

DR DREYFUSS

I don't want to gloat, but just between us, you had that coming to you.
(*tilts Bud's chin up, examines his eye*)
Tch, tch, tch. Are you going to have a shiner tomorrow. Let me get my bag.
(*he starts out*)

BUD
(*calling after him*)
Don't bother, Doc. It doesn't hurt a bit.

He is on Cloud Nine.

FADE OUT:

FADE IN:

147

INT. NINETEENTH FLOOR – DAY

Bud is coming from the elevators toward his office. He is wearing his chesterfield, bowler, and a pair of dark glasses. He opens the office door, starts in.

INT. BUD'S OFFICE – DAY

Bud crosses directly to the phone, removes his glasses – revealing a swollen left eye. He dials a number.

> BUD
> (*into phone*)
> Mr Sheldrake's office? This is C. C. Baxter. Would you please tell Mr Sheldrake I'd like to come up and see him? It's rather important. Will you call me back, please?

He hangs up, takes off his hat and coat, deposits them on the clothes-tree. Then he paces around the office, rehearsing a speech out loud.

> Mr Sheldrake, I've got good news for you. All your troubles are over. I'm going to take Miss Kubelik off your hands.
> (*nods to himself with satisfaction*)
> The plain fact is, Mr Sheldrake, that I love her. I haven't told her yet, but I thought you should be the first to know. After all, you don't really want her, and I do, and although it may sound presumptuous, she needs somebody like me. So I think it would be the thing all around –
> (*the phone rings and he picks it up*)
> – solution-wise.
> (*into phone.*)
> Yes? I'll be right up.

He hangs up, crosses to the door, opens it.

> (*to himself*)
> Mr Sheldrake, I've got good news for you –

Putting on his dark glasses, he heads for the elevators, still talking to himself.

INT. NINETEENTH FLOOR – DAY

Kirkeby and Dobisch are just stepping out of an elevator when Bud approaches. They grin smugly when they see that he is wearing dark glasses.

> KIRKEBY
> Hi, Buddy-boy. What happened to you?

> DOBISCH
> Hit by a swinging door? Or maybe a yellow cab?

Bud pays no attention, walks right past them into the elevator, still muttering to himself. The doors close.

> KIRKEBY
> (*as they move away from the elevators*)
> That guy really must've belted him.

> DOBISCH
> Yeah, he's punchy. Talking to himself.

INT. TWENTY-SEVENTH FLOOR FOYER – DAY

The elevator doors open.

> ELEVATOR OPERATOR
> Twenty-seven.

Bud steps out. As he heads for Sheldrake's office, he continues rehearsing his speech.

> BUD
> You see, Mr Sheldrake, those two days she spent in the apartment – it made me realize how lonely I'd been before. But thanks to you, I'm in a financial position to marry her – if I can ever square things with her family.

He opens the door to Sheldrake's anteroom.

INT. SHELDRAKE'S OFFICE – DAY

Sheldrake is pacing in front of his desk. A couple of suitcases are standing in a corner of the room. The intercom buzzes, and Sheldrake presses the lever down.

Mr Baxter is here.

SHELDRAKE

Send him in.

A beat, then the door opens, and Bud marches in determinedly.

BUD

Mr Sheldrake, I've got good news for you –

SHELDRAKE

And I've got good news for you, Baxter. All your troubles are over.

BUD
(*reacting to the echo*)

Sir?

SHELDRAKE

I know how worried you were about Miss Kubelik – well, stop worrying – I'm going to take her off your hands.

BUD
(*stunned*)

You're going to take her off *my* hands?

SHELDRAKE

That's right.
(*indicating suitcases*)
I've moved out of my house – I'm going to be staying in town, at the Athletic Club.

BUD

You left your wife?

SHELDRAKE

Well, if you must know – I fired my secretary, my secretary got to my wife, and my wife fired me. Ain't that a kick in the head?

BUD

Yeah –

SHELDRAKE

Now what was your news, Baxter?

                    BUD
              (*recovering with difficulty*)
It's about Miss Kubelik – she's all right again – so she went
back home.

                  SHELDRAKE
Swell. And don't think I've forgotten what you did for me.
              (*opens door to adjoining office*)
This way, Baxter.

Bud advances slowly toward the door.

INT. ADJOINING OFFICE – DAY

*It is a slightly smaller and less lavish edition of Sheldrake's office.
Sheldrake ushers Bud through the door, points to the chair behind the
desk.*

                  SHELDRAKE
Sit down. Try it on for size.

Bud obeys like an automaton, lowers himself into the chair.

You like?
              (*indicating office*)
It's all yours.

                    BUD
Mine?

                  SHELDRAKE
My assistant, Roy Thompson, has been shifted to the Denver
office, and you're taking his place.
              (*no reaction from Bud*)
What's the matter, Baxter? You don't seem very excited.

                    BUD
Well, it's just that so many things have been happening so fast
– I'm *very* pleased – especially for Miss Kubelik. Now that
I've gotten to know her better, I think she's the kind of girl
that definitely ought to be married to *somebody* –

Oh, sure, sure. But first the property settlement has to be
worked out – then it takes six weeks in Reno – meanwhile,
I'm going to enjoy being a bachelor for a while.
>   (*starts back toward his own office*)
Oh, by the way, you can now have lunch in the executive
dining room –

BUD

Yes, sir.

He removes his dark glasses reflectively.

SHELDRAKE

That's just one of the privileges that goes with this job. You
also get a nice little expense account, the use of the executive
washroom –
>   (*breaks off, peers at Bud's face*)
Say, what happened to you, Baxter?

BUD

I got kicked in the head, too.

SHELDRAKE

Oh?

*With a shrug, he exits into his own office, closing the door behind him.
Bud sits there, unconsciously bending the glasses in his hand until they
suddenly snap in two. Bud glances down at the two broken halves, as
though surprised by his own violence, tosses them onto the desk.*

DISSOLVE TO:

INT. LOBBY INSURANCE BUILDING – EVENING

*We are close on the building directory. Listed under personnel is
J. D. SHELDRAKE, DIRECTOR, and just below that a man's hand is
inserting the name C. C. BAXTER in the slot marked Asst. Director. The
lettering is complete except for the final R.*

*Camera pulls back to reveal the sign painter we saw earlier, working on
the directory. Watching him is Bud. He is wearing his chesterfield and*

bowler, and still has a slight welt under his left eye. It is after six o'clock, and there is very little activity in the lobby.

Fran, wearing her coat over street clothes, approaches from the direction of the elevators, stops when she sees Bud.

FRAN

Good evening, Mr Baxter.

Bud turns to her in surprise, removes his bowler.

BUD

Oh, Miss Kubelik. How do you feel?

FRAN

Fine. How's your eye?

BUD

Fine.

There is a moment of constraint between them.

FRAN

How's everything at the apartment?

BUD

Nothing's changed. You know, we never finished that gin game –

FRAN

I know.
(*a beat*)
I suppose you heard about Mr Sheldrake – ?

BUD

You mean, leaving his wife? Yeah. I'm very happy for you.

FRAN

I never thought he'd do it.

BUD

I told you all along. You see, you were wrong about Mr Sheldrake.

FRAN

I guess so.

BUD

For that matter, you were wrong about me, too. What you said about those who take and those who get took? Well, Mr Sheldrake wasn't using me – I was using him. See?
(*indicating his name on directory*)
Last month I was at desk 861 on the nineteenth floor – now I'm on the twenty-seventh floor, panelled office, three windows – so it all worked out fine – we're both getting what we want.

FRAN

Yes.
(*looks at her watch*)
You walking to the subway?

BUD

No, thank you.
(*fumbling*)
I – well, to tell you the truth –
(*glancing around lobby*)
– I have this heavy date for tonight –

He points off toward the news-stand. Standing there is a tall, attractive brunette, obviously waiting for someone. Fran looks off in the indicated direction.

FRAN

Oh.

BUD

Aren't you meeting Mr Sheldrake?

FRAN

No. You know how people talk. So I decided it would be better if we didn't see each other till everything is settled, divorce-wise.

BUD

That's very wise.

FRAN

Good night, Mr Baxter.

BUD

Good night, Miss Kubelik.

Fran walks toward the revolving door. Bud watches her for a moment, then strides briskly across the lobby toward the news-stand. He goes right past the waiting brunette, stops in front of a rack of pocket books, examines the merchandise. A man now comes out of a phone booth, joins the waiting brunette, and they go off together. Bud picks out a couple of paperbacks, pays the clerk behind the counter. Stuffing a book into each coat pocket, he moves slowly toward the revolving doors.

DISSOLVE TO:

INT. SHELDRAKE'S OFFICE – DAY

Sheldrake is swivelled around sideways behind his desk, with a bootblack kneeling in front of him, shining his shoes. Reaching for the intercom, Sheldrake presses down one of the levers.

SHELDRAKE

Baxter – would you mind stepping in here for a minute?

BAXTER'S VOICE

Yes, Mr Sheldrake.

The bootblack finishes the second shoe with a flourish, gathers up his equipment. Sheldrake tosses him a half dollar.

BOOTBLACK

Much obliged.

He exits into the anteroom as the door of the adjoining office opens and Bud comes in, carrying several charts. There is no trace left of his black eye.

BUD

(*putting charts on desk*)

Here's the breakdown of figures on personnel turnover. Thirty-seven percent of our female employees leave to get married, twenty-two percent quit because –

SHELDRAKE
(*breaking in*)
You're working too hard, Baxter. It's New Year's Eve – relax.

BUD
Yes, sir.

SHELDRAKE
I suppose you'll be on the town tonight – celebrating?

BUD
Naturally.

SHELDRAKE
Me, too. I'm taking Miss Kubelik out – I finally talked her into it –

BUD
I see.

SHELDRAKE
The only thing is I'm staying at the Athletic Club – and it's strictly stag – so if you don't mind –

BUD
Don't mind what?

SHELDRAKE
You know that other key to your apartment – well, when we had that little scare about Miss Kubelik, I thought I'd better get rid of it quick – so I threw it out the window of the commuter train.

BUD
Very clever.

SHELDRAKE
Now I'll have to borrow your key.

BUD
Sorry, Mr Sheldrake.

SHELDRAKE
What do you mean, sorry?

                                BUD
You're not going to bring anybody up to my apartment.

                            SHELDRAKE
I'm not just bringing *anybody* – I'm bringing Miss Kubelik.

                                BUD
Especially not Miss Kubelik.

                            SHELDRAKE
How's that again?

                                BUD
                             (*flatly*)
No key!

                            SHELDRAKE
Baxter, I picked you for my team because I thought you were
a bright young man. You realize what you're doing? Not to
me – but to yourself. Normally it takes years to work your way
up to the twenty-seventh floor – but it takes only thirty
seconds to be out on the street again. You dig?

                                BUD
                         (*nodding slowly*)
I dig.

                            SHELDRAKE
So what's it going to be?

*Without taking his eyes off Sheldrake, Bud reaches into his pocket,
fishes out a key, drops it on the desk.*

Now you're being bright!

                                BUD
Thank you, sir.

He turns abruptly, starts back into his own office.

INT. BUD'S NEW OFFICE – DAY

*Bud comes in, shutting the door behind him, stands rooted to the spot for
a moment. Then he takes some pencils out of his breast pocket and drops*

*them into a container on the desk, closes his account book, slams a
couple of open file drawers shut.*

*As he crosses to the clothes closet, the connecting door opens and
Sheldrake comes in, key in hand.*

SHELDRAKE

Say, Baxter – you gave me the wrong key.

BUD

No I didn't.

SHELDRAKE
(holding it out)

But this is the key to the executive washroom.

BUD

That's right, Mr Sheldrake. I won't be needing it – because
I'm all washed up around here.

*He has taken his chesterfield and bowler out of the closet, and is putting
the coat on.*

SHELDRAKE

What's gotten into you, Baxter?

BUD

Just following doctor's orders. I've decided to become a
mensch. You know what that means? A human being.

SHELDRAKE

Now hold on, Baxter –

BUD

Save it. The old payola won't work any more. Goodbye, Mr
Sheldrake.

He opens the door to the anteroom, starts out.

INT. SHELDRAKE'S ANTEROOM – DAY

*Bud comes out of his office, carrying his bowler, strides past the
secretaries and through the glass doors to the foyer. An elevator is just
unloading, and beside it a handyman is cleaning out one of the cigarette
receptacles. Bud crosses to the elevator, and as he passes the handyman,
he jams his bowler on the man's head – surrendering his crown, so to
speak. The elevator doors close. The handyman straightens up, looks
around in bewilderment.*

DISSOLVE TO:

INT. THE APARTMENT – NIGHT

*Bud is in the process of packing. In the middle of the living room are
several large cardboard cartons filled with his possessions. The art
posters are off the walls, the bric-à-brac has been removed from the
shelves, and Bud is stowing away the last of his books and records. He
crosses to the fireplace, opens one of the drawers in the cabinet above it,
takes out a fifty-five automatic. He holds the gun in the palm of his
hand, studies it appraisingly. The doorbell rings. Bud snaps out of his
reverie, drops the gun into one of the cartons, goes to the door and opens
it. Standing outside is Dr Dreyfuss, with a plastic ice bucket in his
hand.*

DR DREYFUSS

Say, Baxter – we're having a little party and we ran out of ice
– so I was wondering –

BUD

Sure, Doc.

DR DREYFUSS
(*stepping inside*)
How come you're alone on New Year's Eve?

BUD

Well, I have things to do –

DR DREYFUSS
(*noticing cartons*)
What's this – you packing?

BUD

Yeah – I'm giving up the apartment.

He goes into the kitchen, opens the refrigerator, starts to pry out the ice-cube trays.

DR DREYFUSS

Where are you moving to?

BUD

I don't know. All I know is I got to get out of this place.

DR DREYFUSS

Sorry to lose you, Baxter.

BUD

Me? Oh, you mean my body. Don't worry, Doc – it'll go to
the University – I'll put it in writing –

*He dumps the ice cubes, still in their trays, into the bucket Dr Dreyfuss is
holding. Then he pulls Kirkeby's unopened bottle of champagne out of
the refrigerator.*

Can you use a bottle of champagne?

DR DREYFUSS

Booze we don't need. Why don't you join us, Baxter? We got

two brain surgeons, an ear, nose and throat specialist, a
proctologist, and three nurses from Bellevue.

BUD

No, thanks – I don't feel like it. Look, Doc – in case I don't
see you again – how much do I owe you for taking care of that
girl?

DR DREYFUSS

Forget it – I didn't do it as a doctor – I did it as a neighbor.
(stopping in doorway)
By the way, whatever happened to her?

BUD
(airily)
You know me with girls. Easy come, easy go. Goodbye, Doc.

DR DREYFUSS

Happy New Year.

*Bud closes the door, returns to the kitchen, brings out a box of glassware
and the tennis racquet. As he starts to deposit the racquet in a carton, he
notices a strand of spaghetti clinging to the strings. He removes it gently,
stands there twirling the limp spaghetti absently around his finger.*

CUT TO:

INT. CHINESE RESTAURANT – NIGHT

*It is five minutes before midnight, New Year's Eve. Sitting alone in the
last booth is Fran, a paper hat on her head, a pensive look on her face.
There are two champagne glasses on the table, and the usual
noisemakers, but the chair opposite her is empty. Above the general
hubbub, the Chinese pianist can be heard playing. After a moment,
Fran glances off.*

*Threading his way through the merrymakers crowding the bar and
overflowing from the booths is Sheldrake. He is in dinner clothes, topped
by a paper hat. Reaching the last booth, he drops into the chair facing
Fran.*

SHELDRAKE

Sorry it took me so long on the phone. But we're all set.

161

FRAN

All set for what?

SHELDRAKE

I rented a car – it's going to be here at one o'clock – we're
driving to Atlantic City.

FRAN

Atlantic City?

SHELDRAKE

I know it's a drag – but you can't find a hotel room in town –
not on New Year's Eve.

FRAN
(*a long look at Sheldrake*)
Ring out the old year, ring in the new. Ring-a-ding-ding.

SHELDRAKE

I didn't plan it this way, Fran – actually, it's all Baxter's fault.

FRAN

Baxter?

SHELDRAKE

He wouldn't give me the key to the apartment.

FRAN

He wouldn't.

SHELDRAKE

Just walked out on me – quit – threw that big fat job right in
my face.

FRAN
(*a faint smile*)
The nerve.

SHELDRAKE

That little punk – after all I did for him! He said I couldn't
bring anybody to his apartment – especially not Miss Kubelik.
What's he got against you, anyway?

FRAN
(*a faraway look in her eye*)
I don't know. I guess that's the way it crumbles – cookie-wise.

SHELDRAKE
What are you talking about?

FRAN
I'd spell it out for you – only I can't spell.

The piano player is consulting the watch on his upraised left arm. He drops the arm in a signal, and the lights go out. At the same time, he strikes up 'Auld Lang Syne'.

All over the dimly lit room, couples get to their feet, embracing and joining in the song.

In the last booth, Sheldrake leans across the table, kisses Fran.

SHELDRAKE
Happy New Year, Fran.

Fran's expression is preoccupied. Sheldrake faces in the direction of the pianist, and holding his glass aloft, sings along with the others.

As 'Auld Lang Syne' comes to an end, the place explodes noisily – there is a din of horns, ratchets, and shouted greetings. The lights come up again.

In the last booth, Sheldrake turns back toward Fran – but she is no longer there. Her paper hat lies abandoned on her vacated chair.

Fran –
(*looking around*)
– where are you, Fran?

He rises, cranes his neck, trying to spot her in the crowd.

DISSOLVE TO:

EXT. BROWNSTONE HOUSE – NIGHT

Fran, a coat thrown over the dress she was wearing at the Rickshaw, comes down the street almost at a run. There is a happy, expectant look on her face. She hurries up the steps of the house and through the front door.

INT. STAIRCASE AND SECOND FLOOR LANDING – NIGHT

Fran mounts the stairs eagerly. As she reaches the landing and heads for Bud's apartment, there is a loud, sharp report from inside.

Fran freezes momentarily, then rushes to the door.

> FRAN

Mr Baxter!
> (*pounding on door*)

Mr Baxter! *Mr Baxter!*

The door opens and there stands Bud, the bottle of champagne he has just uncorked still foaming over in his hand. He stares at Fran unbelievingly.

> (*sagging with relief*)

Are you all right?

> BUD

I'm fine.

> FRAN

Are you sure? How's your knee?

> BUD

I'm fine all over.

> FRAN

Mind if I come in?

> BUD
> (*still stunned*)

Of course not.

INT. THE APARTMENT – NIGHT

Fran comes in and Bud shuts the door. The room is the same as we left it, except for an empty champagne glass standing on the coffee table.

> BUD

Let me get another glass.

He goes to one of the cartons, takes out a champagne glass wrapped in newspaper, starts to unwrap it.

FRAN
(*looking around*)

Where are you going?

BUD

Who knows? Another neighborhood – another town – another job – I'm on my own.

FRAN

That's funny – so am I.
(*Bud, pouring champagne, looks up at her*)
What did you do with the cards?

BUD
(*indicating carton*)

In there.

Fran takes the deck of cards and the gin rummy score pad out of the carton, settles herself on the couch, starts to shuffle the cards expertly.

What about Mr Sheldrake?

FRAN

I'm going to send him a fruit cake every Christmas.

Bud sinks down happily on the couch, and Fran holds out the deck to him.

Cut.

Bud cuts a card, but doesn't look at it.

BUD

I love you, Miss Kubelik.

FRAN
(*cutting a card*)

Seven –
(*looking at Bud's card*)
– queen.

She hands the deck to Bud.

165

BUD

Did you hear what I said, Miss Kubelik? I absolutely adore you.

FRAN
(smiling)

Shut up and deal!

Bud begins to deal, never taking his eyes off her. Fran removes her coat, starts picking up her cards and arranging them. Bud, a look of pure joy on his face, deals – and deals – and keeps dealing.

And that's about it. Story-wise.

FADE OUT.

THE END